a SAVOR THE SOUTH *cookbook*

Pickles & Preserves

a SAVOR THE SOUTH *cookbook*

Pickles & Preserves

ANDREA WEIGL

The University of North Carolina Press CHAPEL HILL

The paper in this book meets the guidelines for permanence and durability of
the Committee on Production Guidelines for Book Longevity of the Council on
Library Resources.

Library of Congress Cataloging-in-Publication Data
Weigl, Andrea.
Pickles and preserves / by Andrea Weigl.
pages cm — (A savor the South cookbook)
Includes index.
ISBN 978-1-4696-1440-3 (cloth : alk. paper)
ISBN 978-1-4696-7754-5 (pbk. : alk. paper)
ISBN 978-1-4696-1441-0 (ebook)
1. Pickles. 2. Canning and preserving. 3. Cooking,
American—Southern style. I. Title.
TX805.W45 2014
641.4′62—dc23 2013036720

The Pickled Figs and Yellow Squash Pickles recipes in this book have
been reprinted with permission from *Jean Anderson's Preserving Guide*
(Chapel Hill: University of North Carolina Press, 2012).

Contents

a SAVOR THE SOUTH *cookbook*

Pickles & Preserves

Introduction

y year is defined by canning sessions. In the spring, I make strawberry preserves, turning bucketfuls of ripe fruit into a thick syrup with a layer of berries on top. I love the sight of those jeweled jars lined up on the kitchen counter. In the summer, I put up peaches in many forms—pickled, brandied, or as a thick butter. I also make numerous jars of yellow squash pickles, the canned good most requested by my friends, relatives, and neighbors. In the fall, I stalk my neighbors' neglected fig trees, culling a handful of figs at a time to stash in the freezer. Later, I make fig preserves and use some of them in a fig cake famous on North Carolina's Outer Banks. And in the winter, when I have a free day, I dig up the Jerusalem artichokes growing in my backyard and turn those tubers into a bright yellow relish, a spoonful of which adds a vinegary crunch to a grilled hot dog or a bowl of potato salad.

I'm a northerner by birth and a southerner by circumstance. I've spent the last seventeen years in the South and now consider it home. (I joke that I named my daughter Josephine Pearl because I wanted to be a proper southern mama. I also know that I turned a cultural corner when I started to miss sweet tea and being called "ma'am" whenever I traveled north of the Mason-Dixon Line.) My conversion to adopted southerner started via my stomach. I came to love the South through its food: pimento cheese, biscuits and gravy, fried chicken, the many variations of barbecue. Canning furthered my exploration of southern food traditions.

I started, as many canners do, by making strawberry jam. With each success, I gained the confidence to tackle the next canning challenge, from peach preserves to cucumber pickles. I eventually explored the classic recipes entrenched in southern culture: pickled okra, dilly beans, hot pepper jelly. I came to admire the resourcefulness of southern canners who apparently wasted nothing. Inedible watermelon rinds are turned into pickles. Okra ends up in a canning jar as a way to prevent an overabundant crop from going to waste. Pickled green tomatoes and green tomato relish make use of those bitter, hard tomatoes that won't ripen before the first frost. Then there are all those intriguing recipes that take advantage of uncultivated fruits and vegetables, such as mesquite bean jelly, damson plum preserves, and Jerusalem artichoke pickles.

I also learned how communal canning can be. I joined friends in the kitchen to make all that chopping and peeling go faster. We would turn our kitchens into assembly-line operations for an afternoon and then split the jars between us at the end of the day. We also eagerly shared beloved recipes with each other—a fact that is reflected in this book, which includes many recipes from professional chefs, cookbook authors, and fellow avid canners.

That recipe swapping also revealed to me how canning in the South has evolved beyond pickled okra and dilly beans. These days, people are enjoying the convenience of refrigerator pickles and freezer jams. They're taking advantage of the wide array of ingredients now available, which can be seen in a recipe like salt-cured cucumber pickles with shiso leaves, a Japanese herb.

Generations of canners in the South and beyond owe a debt to French inventor Nicolas Appert, a professional cook known as the father of canning. In the late 1790s, he began experimenting with preserving fruits, vegetables, and meats by packing the food into glass bottles that were sealed with cork and heated in a hot-water bath. The French government had offered a cash prize to anyone who came up with a new way to preserve food. Around 1810, Appert won 12,000 francs for his canning method and published a book on his technique. French newspapers at the time praised him, saying Appert "has found a way to fix the seasons; at his establishment, spring, summer and autumn live in bottles," according to Sue Shephard, author of *Pickled, Potted and Canned: How the Art and Science of Food Preserving Changed the World* (New York: Simon & Schuster, 2000). It's worth noting that Appert and other scientists of that era believed his method worked because it removed all the air from the bottles. The truth was not discovered until 1862, when Louis Pasteur proved that heat kills the microorganisms that spoil food, a process we now know as pasteurization.

Canning spread from Europe to the United States in the early 1800s, and the Mason jar was invented here in 1858. The South's longer growing season created a bounty of produce to be preserved, on both plantations and small family farms, especially in the mountain South. Women—white, black, free, enslaved— undertook much of the work of canning and preserving, and for many, it was a source of well-earned pride. After the Civil War, the region's impoverishment made canning a necessity for many families who turned to foraged fruits and berries. In *Southern Food: At Home, on the Road, in History* (Chapel Hill: University of North Carolina Press, 1993), John Egerton writes about a Tennessee man who made a jelly from the red berries of a nonpoisonous variety of sumac bush. And Ann Cashion writes in *The New Encyclopedia of Southern Culture: Foodways* (Chapel Hill: University of North Carolina Press, 2007) that, "tellingly, cookbooks published after the Civil War include recipes utilizing native fruits that grow uncultivated, such as roselle, persimmon, muscadine, crabapple, and pawpaw."

Many recipes also reflect the cultural heritage of the people living in the South. Descendants of Europeans made marmalade. The British Empire's influence can be seen in chutneys made with green tomatoes, peaches, pears, and apples. German immigrants in the Appalachian Mountains made sauerkraut. Floridians still make guava jelly, which was probably introduced to them by Native Americans in Florida and the Caribbean.

Home canning likely reached its peak in the United States in the 1930s and 1940s. After the Great Depression, the Works Progress Administration helped establish community canning centers in an effort to encourage the nation's struggling inhabitants to become more self-sufficient. The centers continued through World War II, a natural fit with that era's victory gardens. Cashion notes in *The New Encyclopedia of Southern Culture: Foodways* that there were 3,600 community canning centers in the United States by 1946, predominantly in the South, especially Virginia, North and South Carolina, Georgia, and Alabama. After the war, many of the canning centers in the North closed, but those in the South remained open, helping a population still fighting poverty.

Today, a canning revival is under way. Blogs are devoted to canning, introductory classes are offered at farmers' markets, and sales of canning supplies are on the rise. Jarden Home Brands, maker of Ball canning supplies, has been reporting double-digit sales increases. And the company's market research shows that the new generation of home canners consists of not rural grandmothers but urban women under the age of fifty-five. (More than 60 percent of the canners who are members of Ball's Facebook community are under the age of forty-four.) This canning resurgence appears to have many causes, including an increased interest in eating seasonally, shopping at farmers' markets, and reducing the preservatives in food. There also seems to be a desire in our technology-laden world to take up the kitchen arts of previous generations and to feel better about what we're feeding our families. Or maybe in these uncertain times we're seeking the comfort and security of a well-stocked pantry.

Despite the renewed popularity of canning, some people are still intimidated by it. Believe me, canning is easier than you think. This book offers baby-step recipes for beginners as well as intriguing recipes for experienced canners. A newbie can use this book to make a strawberry freezer jam without ever turning on the stove and then graduate to refrigerator pickles, butters, and jellies. And no one should be scared off by the food safety and science information contained in this book. I want readers to know the reasons behind safe canning practices so they can understand why they shouldn't deviate from the instructions. The risk of botulism, which scares many people away from canning, is only a concern when pressure-canning meats, poultry, seafood, and low-acid vegetables. This book contains no such recipes. While it's important to follow the recipe instructions to produce canned goods that are safe to eat, canning isn't nearly as frightful an endeavor as many people have been led to believe. With a little effort, you'll soon have a pantry full of delicious canned goods.

My full pantry has taught me that biscuits are better with homemade jam, that you need something pickled to cut through rich, fatty barbecue, and that a bowl of field peas or beans is more delicious with a spoonful of relish. My pantry also affords me some security. With little notice, I can pull together a pickle plate for a potluck, spoon hot pepper jelly over cream cheese on crackers to serve to unexpected guests, or use a jar of jam to make a cake for a last-minute celebration. Plus, I never have to worry about a hostess gift when I get invited to a dinner party or think about what to give family members, friends, co-workers, or my child's teachers during the holidays.

Whatever your reason for picking up this book, whether you're new to canning or you already have a cupboard full of canned goods, I hope you'll join me in the kitchen to enjoy a taste of the South.

Basic Boiling-water Canning Instructions

EQUIPMENT

You'll need the equipment listed below for boiling-water canning. During the spring and summer, I've found that Walmart generally has the best selection of canning products and equipment. Throughout the year, Food Lion and Ace Hardware always have a small selection of canning supplies. You can also order canning supplies online at www.canningpantry.com, www.canningsupply .com, and www.freshpreservingstore.com.

Water-bath canner: This large pot with a lid and a rack is available in a number of materials, including aluminum, stainless steel, and enamel-coated steel. But any large pot can be used as long as it has a tight-fitting lid and is deep enough for the jars to sit on a rack, an inch of water above the jars, and a couple of inches more for briskly boiling water. If you don't have a canning rack, you can use a cake-cooling rack or fasten together seven screw bands (the part of a two-piece canning lid that screws onto a jar) to form a hexagon. To use a canning pot on an electric range, it must have a flat bottom. A water-bath canner with a ridged bottom is only recommended for gas stovetops.

In the summer, I like to place my water-bath canner outside on a propane turkey fryer to avoid heating up the house. The fryer makes the water come to a boil quickly. Just make sure not to leave the canner unattended once processing begins and place the fryer on a stable surface so the pot doesn't tip over. Setting up a table nearby is helpful for loading and unloading the canner.

Canning jars: Buy glass jars specifically designed for canning. Don't reuse mayonnaise, pickle, spaghetti sauce, or other commercial jars for home canning. Those jars are often designed to be used once, so they can shatter. Canning jars can be used indefinitely as long as they aren't chipped or cracked. Canning jars come in a variety of sizes and styles: 4-ounce, half-pint, pint, and quart jars with regular and wide-mouth openings. Many attractive options are now available, including jelly jars with a quilted pattern and squat, rounded half-pint and pint jars.

Two-piece lids: These lids include a flat disc with a sealing compound around the edge and a screw band. The self-sealing lid may only be used once. If you aren't sure if a lid is new, don't use it. Inspect lids for dents, deformities, or defects in the sealing compound. Use only those in good condition. Jarden Home Brands, which produces Ball canning supplies, recommends using lids no later than the season after you buy them. The screw band can be used repeatedly as long as it isn't rusty or bent.

Plastic freezer or refrigerator jars with twist-on lids: These jars are sold in half-pint, pint, and quart sizes. The smallest size is ideal for making refrigerator and freezer jams. Freezer jams will keep for up to a year in the freezer and up to a month in the refrigerator.

Wide-mouth canning funnel: This funnel is specifically designed to use with canning jars. It makes filling jars easier and less messy. It's often sold as part of a set with a jar lifter, lid wand, and bubble remover–headspace tool.

Jar lifter: This device is used to safely lift jars in and out of a water-bath canner.

Lid wand: This plastic tool has a magnet on one end to lift self-sealing lids out of a saucepan of simmering water right before sealing the jars.

Bubble remover–headspace tool: This ingenious gadget allows you to remove air bubbles and accurately measure headspace—

the room between the lid and the top of the brine or soft spread—which is key to ensuring a properly sealed and safe canned good. One end looks like a miniature set of stairs with each step measuring ¼ inch. You can rest the tool on the rim of the jar to measure the headspace. The other end is tapered and can be inserted into the filled jar to release air bubbles before sealing. (A thin spatula also can be used to release air bubbles.)

Other essentials that you'll need:

- A small saucepan filled with an inch or two of water for simmering the self-sealing lids
- A large stainless-steel stockpot or enamel Dutch oven to make the pickles, brines, or preserves
- A large tea strainer or cheesecloth and butcher string to hold spices used to season pickle brines or syrups (to make it easier to remove the spices at the end of cooking)
- A food-safe nonreactive plastic container with a lid for pickle recipes that call for ingredients to sit overnight (I use a 12-quart bucket with a lid that I bought at a restaurant-supply store)
- A ladle to fill jars with preserves, jams, or brines
- A thin spatula to release air bubbles trapped inside jars of pickles or preserves
- A small clean kitchen towel to wipe the jars' rims before sealing
- Old clean towels to cover the countertop when canning and to place the filled jars on to cool after processing
- Pot holders to safely move pots, remove pot lids, and screw bands on filled jars
- A timer or clock to keep track of cooking and processing times

SPECIAL INGREDIENTS

Besides the equipment you'll need for canning, you'll also need some special ingredients. Below is a list of special ingredients you'll find in this cookbook and older cookbooks and where to buy them.

Alum: Potassium aluminum sulfate is an ingredient that older pickle recipes call for as a firming agent. But most modern canning books advise against its use since consuming large amounts can cause nausea or gastrointestinal problems. Instead, experts suggest soaking cucumbers in ice water for 4–5 hours to improve the texture of pickles. One note when working with cucumbers: Be sure to remove the blossom end of the cucumber, which has an undesirable enzyme that can make pickles soft. If you want to experiment with alum, it can be purchased in the spice aisle of most grocery stores or online.

Calcium chloride is a firming agent added to jars of quick-process or fresh-pack pickles before processing. It's sold as Ball Pickle Crisp with other canning supplies.

Pectin is a naturally occurring substance in some fruits, such as apples and oranges. The commercially made powder or liquid derived from apples or citrus fruits helps jams and jellies set. (Commercially made pectin has a bad reputation among some canners because it includes additives and requires a lot more sugar than recipes made without it. Author Linda Ziedrich offers instructions on how to make your own pectin in *The Joy of Jams, Jellies and Other Sweet Preserves* [Boston: Harvard Common Press, 2009].) Commercially made pectin is available in powdered or liquid form, but the two aren't interchangeable. Instant pectin, low-sugar pectin, and no-sugar pectin are also available. Be sure to follow the recipes included with pectin products for the best results.

Pickling lime: Calcium hydroxide will create a crisp pickle. Food-grade pickling lime, which shouldn't be confused with agricultural or burnt lime, is added to water to create a solution for soaking fresh cucumbers or other vegetables for 12–14 hours before pickling them. After soaking, the vegetables must be rinsed with fresh water and soaked in cold water for 1 hour. Repeat this rinsing and soaking twice. Failure to remove excess lime may increase the risk of botulism. Also, when consumed in large amounts, lime can cause gastrointestinal issues. Pickling lime can be purchased at stores that stock canning supplies.

Pickling salt is a pure, granulated salt without any anti-caking agents. Don't use table salt for pickling, since it can cause a cloudy brine. Pickling salt can be bought in the spice aisle at most grocery stores.

HOW TO TEST WHEN JAMS, JELLIES, AND PRESERVES ARE DONE COOKING

Determining when jams, jellies, and preserves are done cooking can be difficult for beginners. For recipes that don't use pectin, there are three methods for testing doneness. I recommend using the temperature test paired with one of the other methods until you become familiar with the visual cues of the spoon or freezer test.

To use the *temperature test*, cook the soft spread until it reaches 220° on a candy thermometer. Be sure that the end of the thermometer is submerged in the jelly but not touching the bottom of the pot. (Note that you should subtract 2° from the temperature for every 1,000 feet you're above sea level.)

The *spoon test* or *sheet test* is best for jellies. Place several spoons in the freezer for at least 10 minutes. Remove one spoon from the freezer, dip it into the boiling spread, and watch how the liquid falls from the spoon. If light and syrupy droplets fall from the spoon, the spread needs to cook longer. After a bit more cooking, test the spread with another cold spoon and you'll see larger and heavier droplets fall separately off the spoon. When the spread has finally gelled, the liquid won't separate into drops but will "sheet" off the spoon.

The *freezer test* or *saucer test* is best for jams, preserves, marmalades, and syrups. Place several small plates or saucers in the freezer to chill for at least 10 minutes. Pour a small amount of the boiling soft spread on a saucer and place it in the freezer for a few minutes. (Be sure to remove the pan from the heat during the test to prevent scorching.) When you can tip the saucer and the soft spread doesn't run, or when you can draw a line through the soft spread with your finger and it remains open for a few seconds, it's done cooking and ready to be processed.

First, gather your equipment: the canner, jars, lids, bands, and tools. Wash the jars, lids, bands, and tools in hot, soapy water and dry with a clean kitchen towel. Place the number of jars you plan to use inside the canner and fill the canner with enough water to cover the jars by 1 inch. Place the canning pot on the stove over high heat, cover with the lid, and bring the water to a boil. (If you can't easily move the water-filled canning pot from the sink to the stove, place the pot on the stove and use a large pitcher to fill it with water.)

Place the self-sealing lids in a small saucepan with the sealing compound facing up. (After a marathon day of canning, I noticed that the lids facing down left rusty rings on the bottom of the saucepan.) Fill the saucepan with enough water to cover the lids. Cover the saucepan, turn the heat to medium-low, and bring to a simmer. The lids must be heated for at least 10 minutes to achieve a vacuum seal.

Make your pickles or preserves. Once they're ready to go into the jars and the water is boiling in the canner, get ready to work.

Use a jar lifter to remove the hot, sterilized jars from the canner, draining out any water, and place them on a clean towel on the countertop. Fill the jars with a ladle, using the headspace tool to make sure you leave the recipe's prescribed space between the top of the food and the inside of the lid.

Use a bubble remover or thin plastic spatula to slowly stir the contents of each jar to release any air bubbles and run the spatula around the inside of the jar, which will make sure the jar seals properly. Don't use a metal knife or tool to remove the air bubbles since it may scratch the glass and cause the jar to break during processing.

Use a clean damp cloth to wipe the rim of each jar. Remove the self-sealing lids from the simmering water with a lid wand and place a lid on each jar. Place a screw band over each lid and turn it until it's tight. Use the jar lifter to place the jars back in the canning pot. If you're using a rack that doesn't space the jars properly, be sure to leave space between the jars and keep the jars away from the sides of the canning pot. Process as long as required in the recipe.

When done, use the jar lifter to remove the jars from the canner and place them several inches apart on a towel-lined counter. You should soon hear the "pop" of the lids sealing, signaling a job well done. Let the jars cool to room temperature and sit undisturbed for 12–24 hours. Check to make sure the lids are properly sealed. Each lid should be concave and shouldn't move when pressed with a finger. Be sure to label each jar with the contents and the date it was canned.

Store canned goods in a cool, dark pantry or cupboard. Most canned goods should be consumed within a year. (Home-canned goods can be consumed after a year, but the quality won't be as good.) All opened canned goods should be stored in the refrigerator and consumed within a month.

THE SCIENCE BEHIND CANNING FOOD SAFELY

To understand the science behind common canning practices, I spoke with Benjamin Chapman, a food safety expert at North Carolina State University, and Elizabeth Andress, who runs the National Center for Home Food Preservation at the University of Georgia. (Andress co-authored *So Easy to Preserve* [Athens: University of Georgia Cooperative Extension, 2006], an invaluable resource.) Here's what I discovered.

To safely can food at home, you can use either a water-bath canner or a pressure canner. A water-bath canner is used to can fruits, tomatoes, pickles, jams, jellies, and preserves. Jars of food are completely covered with boiling water, which starts boiling when it reaches 212°. A pressure canner is used to can vegetables, meats, poultry, and seafood. Jars are placed in 2–3 inches of water inside a pressure canner and heated to a temperature of 240°. Canned food can only be processed at this higher temperature in a pressure canner.

What we're trying to kill with these two canning methods are enzymes that can cause food to decompose, yeasts, molds, and bacteria, especially the bacteria that causes botulism. Enzymes can be killed at 140° and yeasts and molds at 140°–190°, so processing canned food in a 212° boiling-water bath eliminates enzymes, yeasts, and molds. Bacteria can be either a vegetative cell that can be destroyed at boiling-water temperatures or a spore, which can only be killed at higher temperatures. Under certain conditions, like those you find in a jar of meat or vegetables with low acidity and an absence of air, the spores can produce the toxin that causes botulism. Spores can only be killed by the higher temperatures in a pressure canner. No recipes in this book require pressure canning, and all canned vegetables in the book are pickled, creating a high-acid environment that won't let spores germinate. Tomatoes and figs have borderline pH values and therefore require lemon juice or citric acid to increase the acidity so they can be safely canned using a water-bath canner.

So what's happening when you can food using a water-bath canner, according to Chapman and Andress, is that you're killing any microorganisms that could spoil the food and pushing air out of the jar so it creates a vacuum seal when it cools. Everything you do when canning—heating the lids in simmering water so the rubber seal is softened, wiping the rims of the jars, making sure the bands aren't rusted, stirring to release air bubbles, setting the jars apart from each other as they cool—ensures that air properly vents out of the jars, the jars seal correctly, and what you've canned is safe to eat.

Both Chapman and Andress also urge people to steer clear of the following out-of-date or fad canning methods, which aren't considered safe.

Don't use the open-kettle method, which calls for pouring a hot jam, jelly, or vegetable with pickling liquid into hot jars without processing the jars in a boiling-water bath. This method doesn't kill all the microorganisms that can cause spoilage and can create a risk of botulism.

Don't do pill canning, which calls for adding an aspirin to each jar and then using the open-kettle method.

Don't do steam canning, in which jars are placed in a rack in a shallow pan with a dome lid and processed in a small amount of boiling water. This method doesn't produce enough heat to kill the bacteria that causes botulism.

Don't process canned goods in a dishwasher, which only heats the water to about 165°. Likewise, Andress steers people away from the microwave-canning methods of Australian author Isabel Webb. "We haven't tested her process times. We don't know how she came up with them," Andress says.

Don't use old-style jars with zinc lids or bailing wire and glass caps that use flat rubber rings for sealing. These types of jars are no longer recommended for home canning.

Don't seal your jams or jellies with paraffin. Sealing a jar with paraffin doesn't release air bubbles that may contain contaminants. Andress says pinholes can appear in the wax or it can shrink away from the sides of the jars, creating channels for airborne microorganisms to spoil your canned goods.

WHAT TO DO IF . . .

Your jam or jelly doesn't set: There are four reasons why jellies, jams, and preserves don't set: the fruit or juice was overcooked, which lowers the gelling capacity of the pectin; the proportion of sugar to juice or fruit was off; the fruit or juice was undercooked; or there was too little acid.

If you don't want to bother reprocessing the unset jam, jelly, or preserves, do what I do: relabel the canned good as a syrup and tell people to serve it on ice cream or pound cake. If you want to try again, follow the instructions below.

First, make a trial batch. Add 1 (1.75-ounce) box of pectin to ¾ cup cold water in a small saucepan. Bring to a boil and cook for 2 minutes, stirring constantly. Remove from the heat. Add 1 tablespoon of the pectin mixture and 2 tablespoons sugar to 1 cup unset jam or jelly in a small saucepan. Stir to combine. Bring to a boil and cook for 30 seconds, stirring constantly. Remove from the heat. Skim off the foam. Following the boiling-water canning instructions on page 10, pour into a clean, hot, sterilized jar; seal with a lid; and process the jar in a boiling-water bath for the time listed in the original recipe. Let sit for 24 hours. Place the remaining pectin mixture in the refrigerator.

If the trial batch sets, measure the unset jam or jelly and place it in a large saucepan. For each cup of jam or jelly, add 1 tablespoon of the pectin mixture and 2 tablespoons sugar. Stir to combine. Bring to a boil and cook for 30 seconds, stirring constantly. Remove from the heat. Skim off the foam. Following the boiling-water canning instructions on page 10, pour into jars, seal with lids, and process the jars in a boiling-water bath for the time listed in the original recipe. Let sit on the kitchen counter for 12–24 hours to cool.

Your jars don't seal: If you decide to reprocess jars that didn't seal, do so within 24 hours. Remove the bands and check the lids' sealing compound for any distortions or nicks. Replace any flawed lids and reprocess for the amount of time called for in the recipe, following the instructions for boiling-water canning on page 10.

You notice spoilage inside the jars: Carefully discard the jars, wearing gloves in case the seal has broken and the food is leaking out. The botulism toxin can be fatal whether it's eaten or it comes in contact with the skin. Place the canned food in a heavy garbage bag and dispose of it in a place where humans and animals can't get to it.

If you find mold on jellied products, no need to discard the entire jar because the high sugar content prevents the growth of the bacteria that causes botulism. You can scrape off the mold plus about ½ inch more of the jelly and consume what's underneath.

Recommended Resources

Ball Blue Book Guide to Preserving (Daleville, IN: Hearthmark, 2011) is a slim volume that covers the basics and a great volume for beginners.

Ball Complete Book of Home Preserving: 400 Delicious and Creative Recipes for Today, edited by Judi Kingry and Lauren Devine (Toronto: Robert Rose, 2006), is a more comprehensive volume from today's leading maker of canning jars and supplies.

Jean Anderson's Preserving Guide: How to Pickle and Preserve, Can and Freeze, Dry and Store Vegetables and Fruits (Chapel Hill: University of North Carolina Press, 2012) is a go-to resource from the trustworthy cookbook author Jean Anderson.

The Joy of Pickling and *The Joy of Jams, Jellies and Other Sweet Preserves* (Boston: Harvard Common Press, 1998 and 2009, respectively) are two worthy volumes by Linda Ziedrich. Also check out Ziedrich's website, agardenerstable.com.

So Easy to Preserve, 5th edition, revised, by Elizabeth Andress and Judy Harrison (Athens: University of Georgia Cooperative Extension, 2006), can be ordered at http://setp.uga.edu/. Much of the information in the book is available at http://nchfp.uga .edu/publications/publications_uga.html.

Ball's canning website, www.freshpreserving.com, and helpline at 1-800-240-3340 are very helpful. The website of the National Center for Home Food Preservation at the University of Georgia, nchfp.uga.edu, is also a good source of information.

For fun, consider reading these canning blogs: www.foodinjars .com and www.canningacrossamerica.com.

The agents at local county extension offices often offer classes, safety guidelines, and recipes. Some friendly agents have even been known to check out the condition of old pressure canners for the public.

Jams, Jellies, and Preserves

Imagine capturing the seductive fragrance of honeysuckle in a jar. You can actually do that by making the book's opening recipe, Soft Refrigerator Honeysuckle Jelly. The recipes in this section will make sure that your toast, biscuit, or English muffin is never missing a tasty spread, from Peach-Orange Marmalade to Pear Honey. Jams, jellies, and preserves can also be poured over ice cream, fresh fruit, and cake and can be served as a sweet counterpoint to grilled pork chops and seafood.

Soft Refrigerator Honeysuckle Jelly

I can tell when the honeysuckle is in bloom. I catch whiffs of it traveling on the wind through the open car windows when I'm driving or in the evening when I'm sitting on my screened porch. I was inspired to use those fragrant flowers to create a jelly by chef Bill Smith. Each spring, Bill uses honeysuckle blossoms to make a sorbet that he serves at Crook's Corner restaurant in Chapel Hill, North Carolina. One taste of that sorbet transports people. It takes me back to being a gangly nine-year-old searching out honey-suckle blossoms to suck the sweetness inside. (The children in my neighborhood call them honey suckers.) For Bill's recipe, check out his cookbook, Seasoned in the South: Recipes from Crook's Corner and from Home *(New York: Workman, 2006). After many experiments, I discovered that I could use a honeysuckle infu-sion, as Bill does in his sorbet, to make a jelly. This recipe makes more honeysuckle infusion than you'll need for the jelly. I use the leftover infusion to make lemonade. This jelly is delicious poured over fresh sliced peaches.*

MAKES 2 HALF-PINT JARS

---

4 cups honeysuckle blossoms, packed but not crushed,
   green parts removed, including leaves and tips
5⅓ cups cool water
Juice of half a large lemon
⅔ cup sugar
4 tablespoons instant pectin (also called no-cook
   freezer pectin)

Place the honeysuckle blossoms in a large nonreactive bowl and add the water. Use a plate to weigh down the flowers so they're completely submerged. Let sit out overnight.

The next day, strain the juice from the blossoms and reserve. Measure out 1⅔ cups honeysuckle infusion and place in a bowl. Add the lemon juice.

Combine the sugar and pectin in a large bowl. Stir to prevent lumps of pectin in the jelly.

Pour the honeysuckle mixture into the bowl with the pectin and sugar. Stir briskly with a whisk for 4 minutes until the mixture is thoroughly combined and starts to thicken.

Ladle the jelly into clean plastic freezer jars, seal with lids, and place in the refrigerator. The jelly will be soft set after 24 hours and will keep for 1 month in the refrigerator.

Strawberry Preserves

This is one of those old-fashioned recipes that don't use pectin, so it can be difficult to get the preserves to set. That's OK, though, because if they don't set, what you're left with are delicate ruby berries suspended in a jewel-toned syrup that makes a delicious topping for ice cream, pound cake, or pancakes. My family and friends love to receive these preserves as a gift around the holidays. April McGreger of Farmer's Daughter Brand, a Carrboro, North Carolina, company that makes pickles and preserves using local produce, shared with me her method of ensuring that strawberry preserves set without adding pectin. She said that since ripe strawberries have little pectin, you need to use a mixture of ripe and unripe berries.

MAKES 5 HALF-PINT JARS

2½ pounds whole strawberries, stems removed

4 cups sugar

¼ cup fresh lemon juice, divided

Layer the strawberries and sugar in a large stainless-steel stock-pot or enamel Dutch oven. Pour 2 tablespoons lemon juice over the berries. Let the berries sit for 30 minutes until the juices start to flow.

Place the berries on the stove over medium-low heat. Stir gently until the sugar is fully dissolved, about 10 minutes. Bring to a boil and cook for 3 minutes. Skim off any foam. Remove the berries from the heat and let stand overnight.

The next day, use a slotted spoon to remove the berries to a bowl. Drain any juice back into the pot. Set the berries aside.

Put the syrup back on medium heat. Skim off any foam as it appears. Heat to 220° on a candy thermometer. Add the berries and remaining 2 tablespoons lemon juice to the syrup. Bring back to 220°.

Ladle the strawberries and syrup into hot, sterilized jars, leaving ¼ inch of headspace. Follow the instructions for boiling-water canning on page 10. Process the jars for 10 minutes. These preserves can be enjoyed immediately.

Strawberry–Rose Petal Jelly

I love this delicate jelly on my morning toast or on slices of angel food or sponge cake with fresh sliced strawberries. My friend Jill Warren Lucas of Raleigh, North Carolina, shared this recipe with me, along with a few words of advice: Know the source of the roses. You don't want roses that have been sprayed with chemicals. You also want large, open blooms, free of blemishes and bugs. This recipe makes enough for two batches. Don't try to do it all in one batch; it likely won't set.

MAKES 12 HALF-PINT JARS

6 cups water
3 tablespoons fresh lemon juice, divided
12–15 roses
4½ cups whole strawberries
Juice of 1 large lemon
½ cup white wine
2 (1.75-ounce) boxes of pectin, divided
1 teaspoon butter, divided
9 cups sugar, divided

Place the water and 1 tablespoon lemon juice in a medium stainless-steel saucepan. Gently remove the petals from the roses and add them to the water. Bring to a boil, then reduce the heat and simmer, partially covered, for about 20 minutes. The result should be fragrant, rose-tinted water with color-drained petals that look like wet tissue paper. Move the pan off the heat, cover, and steep for 30 minutes.

While the petals are steeping, clean and trim the strawberries. Either coarsely chop the strawberries or use a food processor to pulse them until chunky but juicy. The chopped berries should measure about 3 cups.

Add the strawberries and remaining 2 tablespoons lemon juice to the rose water and return the mixture to a boil. Reduce the heat and simmer, partially covered, about 10 minutes. Let the mixture cool completely, then cover and refrigerate overnight.

The next day, remove the strawberry–rose petal mixture from the refrigerator and leave on the counter until the contents are at room temperature. Carefully transfer the mixture to a jelly bag or cheesecloth-lined colander set over a bowl. Resist the urge to squeeze the bag or press the contents in the colander to speed up the process of draining the juice as it will result in a cloudy jelly. After about 1 hour, there should be about 6½ cups juice. Add the juice of 1 lemon, the white wine, and enough water to measure 7½ cups total.

Pour 3¾ cups strawberry–rose petal juice into a wide heavy-bottom canning pot or Dutch oven over medium heat. Stir in 1 box of pectin while bringing the jelly to a boil. Add ½ teaspoon butter to reduce the foam.

When the jelly comes to a rolling boil, add 4½ cups sugar all at once, stirring well to combine. Stir frequently until it comes to a rolling boil that can't be stirred down, then let it cook for 1 minute.

Take the pot off the heat and use a spoon to skim off any foam. Ladle the jelly into 6 hot, sterilized jars, leaving ½ inch of headspace. Follow the instructions for boiling-water canning on page 10. Process the jars for 10 minutes. Follow the instructions above to make a second batch using the remaining 3¾ cups strawberry–rose petal juice.

Strawberry Freezer Jam

What I love about this recipe is that it requires so little effort. In thirty minutes, without turning on the stove, you can have several jars of strawberry jam to tuck away in the freezer. I love to fold spoonfuls of this jam into Greek yogurt or slather it on biscuits.

MAKES 4 HALF-PINT JARS

1½ pints whole strawberries, stems removed, cut in half
1 teaspoon fresh lemon juice
1 (1.75-ounce) box of pectin
½ cup light corn syrup
2 cups sugar, divided

Place the strawberries and lemon juice in a large bowl. Use a potato masher or pastry cutter to mash the berries. Add the pectin, stir to combine, and let sit for 20 minutes.

In a large glass measuring cup, microwave the corn syrup on high for 1 minute until simmering. Add 1 cup sugar and stir to combine. Microwave on high for 30 seconds to 1 minute. Add the remaining 1 cup sugar, stir to combine, and microwave again for 30 seconds. Stir again to make sure all the sugar is wet. Add to the strawberries and stir continuously to dissolve the sugar, about 5 minutes.

Pour the jam into clean plastic freezer jars, leaving ½ inch of headspace. Seal with lids and let the jars stand at room temperature until thickened, about 30 minutes. The jam can then be stored in the freezer for up to 1 year. Thaw in the refrigerator before using. Once thawed, enjoy within 1 month.

Peach Butter

You can use fresh or frozen peaches to make this butter. For me, it was a great way to use up peaches that I had ambitiously frozen in June and July but had left languishing in the freezer. My daughter loves this butter spread on her morning waffles.

MAKES 7 HALF-PINT JARS

3½ pounds sliced peaches
Zest and juice of 1 large lemon
½ cup water
2 (¼-inch) slices of fresh peeled ginger
1 cinnamon stick
4 cups sugar
2 tablespoons Grand Marnier or other orange liqueur

Bring the peaches, lemon zest and juice, and water to a boil in a large stainless-steel stockpot or enamel Dutch oven. Remove the pot from the heat.

Purée a few cups of the peaches at a time in a food processor, retaining some texture; don't liquefy them. You'll end up with about 8 cups of purée.

Place the ginger slices and cinnamon stick in several layers of cheesecloth tied with butcher string or in a large tea strainer. Place the spices, peach purée, sugar, and Grand Marnier or other liqueur back into the stockpot or Dutch oven. Bring to a boil and stir to dissolve the sugar. Cook until the butter reaches 220° on a candy thermometer, 35–40 minutes. Remove the spice bag or tea strainer.

Ladle the butter into hot, sterilized jars, leaving ¼ inch of headspace. Follow the instructions for boiling-water canning on page 10. Process the jars for 10 minutes. This butter can be enjoyed immediately.

Peach-Orange Marmalade

The luscious peaches and fragrant oranges in this marmalade complement without overpowering each other. I love to pair this spread with plain buttered scones right out of the oven. This recipe is adapted from one that appears in Damon Lee Fowler's Classical Southern Cooking: A Celebration of the Cuisine of the Old South *(New York: Crown Publishers, 1995). Fowler notes that it isn't a true marmalade but more like a fruit conserve or butter. The original recipe was called a marmalade in nineteenth-century cookbooks. Fresh peaches will need to be mashed with a wooden spoon or potato masher while cooking, although this is not necessary if you use frozen peaches.*

MAKES 3 HALF-PINT JARS

About 2 pounds freestone peaches, peeled, pitted, and sliced

2 cups sugar

2 oranges

$\frac{1}{2}$ cup water, plus more if needed

Place the peaches and sugar in a large stainless-steel stockpot or enamel Dutch oven.

Wash the oranges well. Using a vegetable peeler, remove thin strips of peel from the oranges without including the white pith. Set the peel aside. Using a paring knife, cut off the white pith from the oranges and separate the sections from the membranes. Discard the seeds. Chop the orange sections and add them to the peaches.

Squeeze whatever juice is left in the orange membranes into the pot with the peaches. Mince the orange peel and add it to the peaches.

Bring the peaches to a boil and stir to dissolve the sugar. Reduce to a simmer. When the peaches are tender enough, break them up with a potato masher. Cook until you get the thickness you desire, similar to an apple or peach butter, stirring often. This can take 1–2 hours. Add water, ¼ cup at a time, if needed to make sure the marmalade doesn't scorch.

Ladle the marmalade into hot, sterilized jars, leaving ¼ inch of headspace. Follow the instructions for boiling-water canning on page 10. Process the jars for 10 minutes.

Peach and Blueberry Freezer Jam

I love to pull a jar of this jam out of the freezer on a dreary winter day. The taste of peaches and blueberries reminds me of summer. Savoring this jam on buttered whole wheat toast or an English muffin helps me remember that no matter how cold the weather is, it won't last forever.

MAKES 5 PINT JARS

1 cup blueberries

1½ cups sugar

1 (1.59-ounce) pouch instant pectin (also called
    no-cook freezer pectin)

3 cups finely chopped peeled peaches

1 teaspoon fresh lemon juice

Place the blueberries in a microwave-safe bowl and microwave on high for about 2 minutes, stopping several times to stir and crush the berries with the back of a spoon. Continue cooking until the mixture reaches a boil.

Combine the sugar and pectin in a large bowl and stir to break up any lumps. Add the blueberries, peaches, and lemon juice. Stir for 3 minutes.

Ladle the jam into clean plastic freezer jars, leaving ½ inch of headspace. Seal with lids and let the jars stand at room temperature until thickened, about 30 minutes. Enjoy immediately, refrigerate for up to 1 month, or keep in the freezer for up to 1 year.

Blackberry Jam

My husband loves blackberries. There's no question which jar he'll pull out of the refrigerator for his weekday-morning toast or weekend biscuit. If you aren't a fan of the seeds, strain the crushed berries through a fine mesh sieve to remove the seeds.

MAKES 8 HALF-PINT JARS

---

4 pints blackberries
4 cups sugar
½ tablespoon butter
1 (1.75-ounce) box of pectin

Place the blackberries in a large stainless-steel stockpot or enamel Dutch oven and use a potato masher or the back of a large spoon to crush the berries. Turn the heat to medium-high. Add the sugar and stir until the sugar is dissolved. Add the butter.

Bring the berry mixture to a boil. When the boiling is so rapid that stirring doesn't lessen it, add the pectin. Return to a boil and stir constantly for 1 minute.

Ladle the jam into hot, sterilized jars, leaving ¼ inch of headspace. Follow the instructions for boiling-water canning on page 10. Process the jars for 10 minutes.

Damson Plum Preserves

I was dancing with joy at the farmers' market when I spotted damson plums for sale. The dark purple skins set off the yellow flesh, which is too tart for eating but perfect for preserves. The most time-consuming part of this recipe is pitting the plums. Your best chance of getting these preserves to set is with ripe but not overly ripe plums. Even if the preserves don't set, you'll have a wonderful syrup to drizzle over pancakes or scoops of vanilla ice cream.

MAKES 16 HALF-PINT JARS

---

6 pounds damson plums, unpeeled, halved, and pitted

1½ cups water

11 cups sugar

Combine the plums, water, and sugar in a large stainless-steel stockpot or enamel Dutch oven. Cook the preserves over medium-low heat, stirring to dissolve the sugar, until they reach 220° on a candy thermometer.

Ladle the preserves into hot, sterilized jars, leaving ¼ inch of headspace. Follow the instructions for boiling-water canning on page 10. Process the jars for 15 minutes. You can enjoy these preserves immediately.

Muscadine Jam

The muscadine, a native southern grape, grows from Delaware to Texas. Muscadines aren't the best eating grapes because their skin is tough and they're filled with seeds. But if you like their sweet flavor and musky smell—and many southerners and northern transplants do—these grapes make an excellent jam. This jam is a nice complement to grilled pork or roasted venison but is just as lovely on your toast at breakfast.

MAKES 10 HALF-PINT JARS

1 quart muscadine grapes
$\frac{1}{2}$ cup water, plus more if needed
6$\frac{3}{4}$ cups sugar

Separate the grape skins from the pulp by popping the grapes between your thumb and index finger. Place the pulp with the seeds in a medium bowl and the skin in a medium stainless-steel saucepan. Remove the seeds from the pulp, making several passes since it's hard to remove all the seeds on the first attempt.

Add the water to the skins in the saucepan. Cook over medium-high heat, about 30 minutes, or until the skins are tender. Stir occasionally. You may need to add more water, $\frac{1}{2}$ cup at a time, to prevent scorching. When the skins are tender, transfer to a food processor and pulse until finely chopped.

Return the chopped skins to the saucepan. Add the pulp, any accumulated grape juice, and the sugar. Bring to a boil. Cook for about 10 minutes, until the jam reaches 220° on a candy thermometer.

Ladle the jam into hot, sterilized jars, leaving $\frac{1}{4}$ inch of headspace. Follow the instructions for boiling-water canning on page 10. Process the jars for 10 minutes.

Hot Pepper Jelly

You can't consider yourself a true southern cook until you've served this classic appetizer: hot pepper jelly spooned over a block of softened cream cheese with crackers. John Egerton reports in Southern Food: At Home, on the Road, in History *(Chapel Hill: University of North Carolina Press, 1993) that the first recipe he could find for pepper jelly was in the classic cookbook,* Charleston Receipts, *by the Junior League of Charleston, which was first published in 1950. Feel free to use red, orange, green, or purple bell peppers instead of yellow if you like.*

MAKES 7 HALF-PINT JARS

4 jalapeños, seeded and quartered
3 medium yellow bell peppers, quartered
1 cup white vinegar
½ teaspoon hot sauce
6½ cups sugar
½ tablespoon butter
2 (3-ounce) pouches of liquid pectin

Pulse the jalapeños in a food processor until finely diced but not liquefied. Place them in a large stainless-steel stockpot or enamel Dutch oven.

Pulse the bell peppers in the food processor until finely diced but not liquefied and add them to the pot. Add the vinegar, hot sauce, sugar, and butter. Bring the jelly to a boil and stir until the sugar is dissolved. When the boiling is so rapid that stirring doesn't lessen it, add the pectin, stir constantly, and bring back to a boil for 1 minute.

Ladle the jelly into hot, sterilized jars, leaving ¼ inch of headspace. Follow the instructions for boiling-water canning on page 10. Process the jars for 10 minutes.

Habañero Gold Pepper Jelly

This sweet-and-spicy pepper jelly makes an excellent sauce to serve with grilled swordfish or for basting grilled or roasted pork tenderloin. The recipe comes from Rebecca Ashby of Winston-Salem, North Carolina.

MAKES 3 HALF-PINT JARS

½ cup diced dried apricots
¾ cup white vinegar
¼ cup finely chopped red onion
¼ cup finely chopped red bell pepper
½ cup seeded, finely chopped habañero pepper
3 cups sugar
1 (3-ounce) pouch of liquid pectin

Place the apricots and vinegar in a large stainless-steel stockpot or enamel Dutch oven. Let the apricots soak at room temperature for at least 4 hours.

Add the red onion, bell pepper, habañero pepper, and sugar and stir. Bring the mixture to a boil. When the boiling is so rapid that stirring doesn't lessen it, add the pectin. Return to a boil and cook for 1 minute.

Ladle the jelly into hot, sterilized jars, leaving ¼ inch of headspace. Follow the instructions for boiling-water canning on page 10. Process the jars for 10 minutes.

Fig Preserves

Each fall, my neighbor Ralph Whisenant and I stalk our neighbors' fig trees. Our neighbors don't seem to like figs, but these trees grow so well in our subdivision that every third house seems to have one. As fig fans, Ralph and I are lucky. Often, I only get a dozen or so figs at a time. So I wash and dry the figs, cut off the stems, throw the figs into a plastic zip-top bag, and place them in the freezer. I add more figs to the bag as the harvest continues over several weeks. Eventually, I'll have enough to make preserves. I use my store of fig preserves to make Ocracoke Fig Cake, a recipe that can be found in Chapel Hill, North Carolina, food writer Nancie McDermott's Southern Cakes: Sweet and Irresistible Recipes for Everyday Celebrations *(San Francisco: Chronicle Books, 2007). Nancie's version of the moist spice cake—named after the Outer Banks island where my husband and I eloped—is a family favorite.*

MAKES 11 HALF-PINT JARS

5½ pounds figs
1 large lemon
5 cups sugar

Wash the figs and cut off the stems. Place the figs in a large stainless-steel stockpot or enamel Dutch oven. Use a sharp knife or mandolin to thinly slice the lemon. Remove the seeds from the lemon slices. Add the lemon slices and sugar to the figs. Stir to combine.

Bring the fig mixture to a boil over medium-high heat. Stir to dissolve the sugar. Reduce the heat to a simmer and cook for about 1 hour, or until the figs are translucent and the syrup thickens. Cook the preserves until the temperature registers 220° on a candy thermometer.

Ladle the preserves into hot, sterilized jars, leaving ¼ inch of headspace. Follow the instructions for boiling-water canning on page 10. Process the jars for 10 minutes.

Apple Butter

The apple sellers at my local farmers' market insist that the best varieties for making apple butter are Golden Delicious, Rome, and Stayman Winesap. I save time by chopping the cored, peeled apples in a food processor. I learned another trick from Chapel Hill, North Carolina, cookbook author Sheri Castle, who adds a bit of acid at the end of the cooking to enhance the taste of her apple butter. My recipe calls for apple cider vinegar, but Sheri uses lemon juice or balsamic vinegar.

MAKES 3 PINT JARS

½ peck apples, peeled, cored, and chopped

2½ cups apple cider vinegar

4 cups sugar

2 tablespoons sorghum

1 teaspoon cinnamon

¼ cup apple cider vinegar or fresh lemon juice

Place the apples, vinegar, sugar, and sorghum in a large stainless-steel stockpot or enamel Dutch oven. Stir to mix well. Cook over medium-low heat for 2–2½ hours. Stir occasionally to prevent scorching. You'll need to stir more often the longer it cooks.

When the butter is the consistency you like, add the cinnamon and vinegar or lemon juice and stir. Let cook another 5 minutes.

Ladle the butter into hot, sterilized jars, leaving ¼ inch of headspace. Follow the instructions for boiling-water canning on page 10. Process the jars for 10 minutes. This butter can be enjoyed immediately.

Apple and Fig Preserves

Apples and figs make a lovely pair. Marilyn Markel, who shared this recipe with me, runs a cooking school at Southern Season's Charleston, South Carolina, store. Southern Season is a chain of gourmet food and housewares stores that started in Chapel Hill, North Carolina. These preserves are good for slathering on biscuits or as a condiment for grilled pork.

MAKES 8 PINT JARS

1 cup apple cider
6 cups apples, such as Golden Delicious, Rome, or
    Stayman Winesap, peeled, cored, and sliced
½ cup diced dried figs
½ teaspoon butter
1 tablespoon fresh lemon juice
2 cups granulated sugar
2 cups brown sugar
1 (1.75-ounce) box of pectin
½ teaspoon cinnamon
¼ teaspoon nutmeg

Combine the apple cider, apples, figs, butter, and lemon juice in a large stainless-steel stockpot or enamel Dutch oven and bring to a boil. Cook for 10–12 minutes until the apples are tender.

Add the sugars, stirring gently. Add the pectin and bring to a boil for 1 minute. Remove from the heat and stir in the spices.

Ladle the preserves into hot, sterilized jars, leaving ¼ inch of headspace. Follow the instructions for boiling-water canning on page 10. Process the jars for 10 minutes. These preserves can be enjoyed immediately.

Refrigerator Sweet Potato Butter

I—and my daughter—love to spread this citrusy Sweet Potato Butter on our waffles instead of syrup. This recipe was shared with me by Sue Langdon, president of the N.C. Sweet Potato Commission. Did you know that North Carolina produces almost 50 percent of the country's sweet potato crop? That's 960 million pounds of sweet potatoes a year, or 98 pounds per North Carolina resident.

MAKES 3 HALF-PINT JARS

2 medium sweet potatoes
1½ cups orange juice
¼ cup light corn syrup
½ cup sugar
¼ teaspoon ginger
¾ teaspoon cinnamon

Preheat the oven to 350°.

Pierce the sweet potatoes with a fork or knife several times. Place them on a baking sheet and bake for about 1 hour, until they can be easily pierced with a knife. Let cool until you can use your fingers to peel off the skin.

Purée the sweet potatoes in a food processor until smooth. You should end up with about 2 cups of puréed sweet potatoes.

Combine the sweet potatoes, orange juice, corn syrup, sugar, ginger, and cinnamon in a large stainless-steel stockpot or enamel Dutch oven. Mix well. Cook over low heat until thick and smooth, 30–45 minutes.

Ladle the butter into clean plastic freezer jars. You can freeze this butter for up to 1 year or keep it in the refrigerator for up to 1 month.

Pear Honey

I was seduced by the name of this recipe, which kept turning up in old southern cookbooks. Who wouldn't want to eat something called pear honey? Think of it as pear butter and enjoy it slathered on savory cheddar cheese scones.

MAKES 5 PINT JARS

7–8 ripe Bartlett pears, peeled, cored, and sliced
Juice of 1 large lemon
1 (20-ounce) can pineapple chunks with juice
5 cups sugar

If you like smooth preserves, blitz the pears, lemon juice, and pineapple in a food processor and then place the purée in a large stainless-steel stockpot or enamel Dutch oven. Otherwise, use a potato masher to smash the pear slices and pineapple chunks with the lemon juice in the pot.

Add the sugar to the fruit. Stir to combine. Cook on medium-low heat for 1–1½ hours. Adjust the heat if necessary and stir occasionally to prevent burning.

When the pear honey is as thick as you like, ladle it into hot, sterilized jars, leaving ¼ inch of headspace. Follow the boiling-water canning instructions on page 10. Process the jars for 10 minutes. Pear Honey can be enjoyed immediately.

Mesquite Bean Jelly

I love it when recipes come to me via a circuitous path. This is certainly one of those. Raleigh, North Carolina, cookbook author Debbie Moose raved about this jelly, made by a friend of a friend, John Roby of San Antonio, Texas. When I contacted Roby, he sent me the recipe and a jar of the jelly with this note: "Of all my local jellies (loquat, cactus tuna, and mustang grape are the others), friends like this the most because it's unique in flavor and color compared to anything you're likely to eat. 'Honey' and 'vanilla' are the closest words folks come up with to describe the golden spread." The jar that Roby sent me was delicious. It was as if I was tasting a cousin of honey. If you're lucky enough to live close to mesquite trees, give this a try and help spread this Texas foodways tradition.

MAKES 6 PINT JARS

---

3 cups mesquite bean juice
⅓ cup fresh lemon juice
1 (1.75-ounce) box of pectin
4½ cups sugar

Fill a 1-gallon container with mesquite beans when they've turned a tan color and begun to drop from the trees. Immerse the beans in water for a few minutes to remove any bugs, then drain.

Place the beans in a large stainless-steel stockpot or enamel Dutch oven with just enough water to cover the beans. Bring to a boil and cook until the beans are softened, about 10 minutes. Add 3 cups water and soak the softened beans overnight.

The next day, bring the beans back to a boil. Remove the pot from the heat, let cool a bit, then drain the beans in a colander lined with several layers of cheesecloth, reserving the juice.

Combine 3 cups of the mesquite bean juice, the lemon juice, and the pectin in a medium saucepan. Stir. Bring to a full rolling boil that stirring won't lessen. Add the sugar and stir to dissolve. Let return to a full rolling boil for 1 minute.

Ladle the jelly into hot, sterilized jars, leaving ¼ inch of headspace. Follow the instructions for boiling-water canning on page 10. Process the jars for 10 minutes.

Pickles

This chapter is for people who love, almost crave, the sour, tart flavor of a good pickle. The recipes will broaden your pickle horizons. There are Dilly Beans and Pickled Okra, Pickled Figs and Mustard Pickle, which shows off what cauliflower can do as a pickle. Try out a few recipes, and you'll have one heck of a pickle plate to set before dinner guests. Beware—these pickles can steal the show.

Dilly Beans

Southern food doyenne and cookbook author Nathalie Dupree serves her dilly beans wrapped in thin slices of prosciutto or country ham as an appetizer. The key to this recipe is using young, tender beans. You'll be disappointed otherwise.

MAKES 3 PINT JARS

---

3 garlic cloves
¾ teaspoon red pepper flakes
3 teaspoons dried dill weed
1 pound green beans, trimmed to fit the jars
2 cups white vinegar
1½ cups water
1½ tablespoons pickling salt

Place 1 garlic clove, ¼ teaspoon red pepper flakes, and 1 teaspoon dried dill weed in each hot, sterilized jar. Divide the green beans into thirds and pack tightly into the jars.

Place the vinegar, water, and pickling salt in a medium stainless-steel saucepan and bring to a boil. Stir until the salt is dissolved.

Pour the brine over the beans, leaving ¼ inch of headspace. Follow the instructions for boiling-water canning on page 10. Process the jars for 10 minutes. Enjoy these beans after 1 month.

Dill Pickles

I find that calcium chloride, sold by Ball as Pickle Crisp, helps these pickles stay crispy. I like to eat these pickles with ham, turkey, or grilled cheese sandwiches.

MAKES 3 QUART JARS

3 pounds pickling cucumbers, such as Kirby
12 fresh dill fronds
12 garlic cloves
¾ teaspoon calcium chloride
3 cups white vinegar
4½ cups water
2 tablespoons pickling salt
2 teaspoons dill seeds
10 black peppercorns
3 bay leaves

Cut each cucumber in half lengthwise. Place 4 dill fronds, 4 garlic cloves, and ¼ teaspoon calcium chloride in each hot, sterilized jar. Pack the cucumber halves into the jars.

Bring the vinegar, water, pickling salt, dill seeds, peppercorns, and bay leaves to a boil in a medium stainless-steel saucepan. Stir to dissolve the salt.

Ladle the brine into the jars to cover the cucumbers, leaving ½ inch of headspace. Follow the instructions for boiling-water canning on page 10. Process for 15 minutes. Let the pickles sit for 1 month before opening.

Spicy and Sour Refrigerator Pickles

I don't think my husband and I could survive without a jar or two of pickles in the refrigerator to serve with hamburgers, hot dogs, and pulled pork sandwiches. So it really says something that this recipe has become our go-to recipe for cucumber pickles. I've even used the same brine to pickle jalapeño slices. I first tasted these pickles while judging a cooking contest at Burt's Bees corporate headquarters in Durham, North Carolina. The recipe is adapted from Beth Ritter's winning entry. Ritter says it appeared in the Fort Worth Star-Telegram *years ago and was attributed to Dock and Opal Everett, who used to own a produce stand in Waco, Texas. I use a mandolin to make quick work of slicing the cucumbers, jalapeño, and onion.*

MAKES 2 QUART JARS

2 pounds pickling cucumbers, such as Kirby,
    cut into ¼-inch slices
1 jalapeño, seeded and sliced
1 onion, sliced
4 cups white vinegar
¼ cup pickling salt
3½ cups sugar
1½ teaspoons celery seeds
1½ teaspoons turmeric
1½ teaspoons mustard seeds
1 tablespoon black peppercorns

Combine the cucumbers, jalapeño, and onion in a large bowl.

Heat the vinegar, pickling salt, sugar, celery seeds, turmeric, mustard seeds, and peppercorns in a medium stainless-steel saucepan over medium-low heat. Stir until the sugar and salt are dissolved, about 10 minutes.

Pack the vegetables evenly into hot, sterilized jars. Ladle the brine over the pickles, leaving ½ inch of headspace. Seal the jars with lids.

Let the pickles sit in the refrigerator for 5 days before eating. These pickles are good for 1 year but best within 3 months.

Bread-and-Butter Pickles

Felicia Gressette is my former boss at the News & Observer *in Raleigh, North Carolina. She grew up in St. Matthews, South Carolina, and used to be the food editor at the* Miami Herald. *While I was working on this book, she shared a copy of "The Gressette Family Cookbook" with me. Among the delights in that volume is a recipe for bourbon balls that calls for two corsage pins to use to dip the balls in chocolate. This recipe was inspired by a recipe by Felicia's second cousin, Emily Rucker. I try to always have a jar of these pickles in the refrigerator to serve with grilled bratwurst or on pickle plates.*

MAKES 4 QUART JARS

12–15 pickling cucumbers, such as Kirby,
    cut into ¼-inch slices
3 white onions, cut into ¼-inch slices
½ cup pickling salt
Ice cubes
5 cups apple cider vinegar
5 cups sugar
2 tablespoons mustard seeds
1 teaspoon celery seeds
½ teaspoon turmeric

Place a ½-inch layer of sliced cucumbers in a large bowl. Top with a ½-inch layer of sliced onions. Sprinkle about a fourth of the pickling salt and a handful of ice cubes on top of the vegetables. Repeat the layers of cucumbers, onions, salt, and ice cubes until the bowl is full; you may have to use a second bowl. Let the salted vegetables sit for 3–4 hours.

Bring the vinegar, sugar, mustard seeds, celery seeds, and turmeric to a simmer in a large stainless-steel stockpot or enamel Dutch oven. Stir until the sugar is dissolved, about 10 minutes.

Drain the cucumbers and onions. Remove any ice cubes. Rinse with cold water to remove the salt.

Pack the cucumbers and onions into hot, sterilized jars. Ladle the brine over the vegetables, leaving ½ inch of head-space. Follow the instructions for boiling-water canning on page 10. Process the jars for 10 minutes. These pickles will be ready to eat after 1 month.

Old-Fashioned Crisp Sweet Pickles

People either love or hate these pickles; there is no in-between. I adore a crisp pickle and therefore love them. My husband likes a softer pickle and so despises the texture of these. This recipe comes from Nancy Smith, a New Bern, North Carolina, native. Nancy got the recipe from her mother and has been making these pickles for more than forty years. There are two keys to this recipe: use small cucumbers, which have fewer seeds, and cut the cucumbers into thick, ½-inch slices. Thinner slices or slices from larger cucumbers with more seeds tend to break after sitting for as long as forty-eight hours, first in pickling lime, then in brine. Thicker slices from smaller cucumbers can survive the stirring, rinsing, cooking, and packing. For people who love these pickles, a jar won't last long in the refrigerator.

I went to a local restaurant-supply store to buy a twelve-quart food-safe plastic bucket with a lid to make these pickles, but any food-safe nonreactive container with a lid will work. When using pickling lime, avoid aluminum containers, colanders, and pots because the lime can react with the metal, increasing the aluminum content of the pickles, according to the National Center for Home Food Preservation at the University of Georgia.

MAKES 7 PINT JARS

1½ cups pickling lime, such as Mrs. Wage's

1 gallon water

3½ pounds pickling cucumbers, such as Kirby,
   cut into ½-inch slices

9 cups sugar

4 cups apple cider vinegar

4 cups water

1 teaspoon whole allspice

½ cinnamon stick

Combine the pickling lime and 1 gallon water in a large non-reactive container with a lid. Stir to dissolve. Add the cucumbers and place the lid on the container. Let sit 12–24 hours, occasionally shaking the container to disperse the pickling lime that has accumulated on the bottom.

Drain off the lime water. Rinse the cucumbers in a plastic colander. Wash the container that held the cucumbers and refill it with cool water. Place the cucumbers in the container and let sit for 1 hour. Repeat the rinsing and soaking twice more. Place the drained cucumbers in the same container.

Mix the sugar, vinegar, and water in a large stainless-steel stockpot or enamel Dutch oven over medium-high heat. Stir to dissolve the sugar. Once the sugar is dissolved, remove from the heat and pour the brine over the cucumbers in the nonreactive container. Cover with the lid. Let sit 12–24 hours.

Transfer the cucumbers and brine into a large stockpot. Place the allspice and cinnamon stick in several layers of cheesecloth tied with butcher string or a large tea strainer and add to the pot. Simmer the pickles for about 1 hour.

Ladle the pickles and brine into hot, sterilized jars. Follow the instructions for boiling-water canning on page 10. Process the jars for 10 minutes. These pickles can be enjoyed after about 1 week.

Salt-Pickled Cucumbers with Shiso

This recipe comes from James Beard Award–winning chef Andrea Reusing of Lantern restaurant in Chapel Hill, North Carolina. Shiso leaves are common in Japanese cuisine and can be found at Asian grocery stores and some farmers' markets. These spicy and sour pickles are a lovely counterpoint to a barbecue sandwich or a batch of chicken wings.

MAKES 5 QUART JARS

---

2 quarts water, divided
¼ cup plus 1 tablespoon kosher salt
30 Sichuan peppercorns (or 10 black peppercorns)
1 head of garlic, unpeeled, cut in half crosswise
2 pounds small pickling cucumbers, such as Kirby,
    stems trimmed
5 purple shiso leaves

In a small saucepan over high heat, bring 2 cups of the water to a boil. Remove from the heat and add the salt, peppercorns, and garlic. Let cool and then add the remaining water.

Place the cucumbers in a large crock or food-safe plastic container, layering them with the shiso leaves. Pour the brine mixture over the cucumbers, covering them completely. Place one or more small plates on top of the cucumbers in order to keep them completely submerged. Cover with a lid. Store in a cool (68°–70° is ideal), dark room for 3 days to a week, checking every day or so to remove any mold or foam that rises to the top. The pickles are done when they're pleasantly sour and tangy but still firm. Store refrigerated for several weeks.

Pickled Ginger

Young or mature ginger can be pickled, but young ginger is best because it's less fibrous. Young ginger has pale skin and pink tips and is only in season from January to the end of spring. Mature ginger is available year-round. Choose ginger that is heavy and firm with smooth, unwrinkled skin. This recipe comes from James Beard Award–winning cookbook author Grace Young, known as the poet laureate of the wok. My favorite of Grace's books is Stir-Frying to the Sky's Edge: The Ultimate Guide to Mastery, with Authentic Recipes and Stories *(New York: Simon & Schuster, 2010). If you do any Asian cooking, it's nice to have homemade pickled ginger on hand.*

MAKES 1 PINT JAR

½ pound fresh ginger
1 cup rice vinegar
⅓ cup sugar
2 teaspoons kosher salt

Peel the ginger with the edge of a teaspoon. Use a mandolin to cut the peeled ginger into scant ⅛-inch slices to make about 2 cups.

In a medium saucepan, bring 3 cups water to a boil over high heat. Add the ginger and cook for 30 seconds. Drain in a colander, shaking well to remove excess water. Pack the ginger into the hot, sterilized jar.

Meanwhile, in a small saucepan, combine the vinegar, sugar, and salt and bring to a boil over high heat, stirring until the sugar and salt are dissolved. Boil for 1 minute.

Carefully pour the hot pickling liquid into the jar. Use chopsticks or a spoon to press down on the ginger to make sure it's covered in pickling liquid. Cover with a clean lid and let stand at room temperature until cool. Refrigerator overnight before using. Pickled ginger will keep refrigerated for 2–3 weeks.

Pickled Peaches

The sweet-and-sour taste of these peaches is excellent with ham or roasted pork. It's traditional to pickle whole clingstone peaches, but cut freestone peaches in half so you can pack more into the jars.

MAKES 3 WIDE-MOUTH QUART JARS

Juice of 3 large lemons
6 pounds peaches
3 cups apple cider vinegar
6 cups light brown sugar
Whole cloves
9 cinnamon sticks
2-inch piece of fresh ginger, peeled and cut into 9 slices

Make sure everything is in place before you get started. Fill a large stainless-steel stockpot or enamel Dutch oven with water and set it on the stove over medium-high heat. While the water is heating, prepare an ice-water bath in a large bowl. In a second large bowl, combine the lemon juice and enough water to cover the peaches after they've been blanched and peeled.

Once the water on the stove is boiling, gently drop a few peaches at a time into the pot. When the peach skin "shrugs" to the touch after a few minutes, use a slotted spoon to remove the peach to the ice-water bath. If the skin doesn't loosen after a few minutes, remove the peach and peel it with a vegetable peeler when it's cool enough to handle. Repeat with the remaining peaches.

Remove the skin from the peaches. If using freestone peaches, cut each peach in half and discard the pits; if using clingstones, leave the peaches whole. Place the peaches in the bowl with the water and lemon juice.

Bring the vinegar and brown sugar to a boil in a large stainless-steel stockpot or enamel Dutch oven. Stir to dissolve the sugar. Lower the heat to a simmer and cook for about 20 minutes, stirring occasionally. Place 8 peach halves or 4 whole peaches at a time in the pot. Simmer until tender or easily pierced by a knife. Remove to a large platter. Stick a whole clove into each peach half or each peach. Repeat with the remaining peaches.

Place 3 cinnamon sticks and 3 slices of ginger in each hot, sterilized jar. Pack the peaches into the jars. Ladle syrup over the peaches in the jars, leaving ½ inch of headspace. Follow the instructions for boiling-water canning on page 10. Process the jars for 15 minutes. Let the pickles sit for 1 month before serving.

Pickled Okra

I love pickled okra, especially served in a bloody mary with olives and gherkins.

MAKES 4 PINT JARS

---

2 pounds medium-sized okra, stems removed, caps on
4 garlic cloves
4 dried red chili peppers, such as árbol
2 cups white vinegar
2 cups water
1½ tablespoons pickling salt

Pack the okra into hot, sterilized jars. Arrange the pods in circles with stems pointing up, then place more okra with stems pointing down into the gaps. Squeeze in more than you think is possible. Add 1 garlic clove and 1 chili pepper to each jar.

Bring the vinegar, water, and pickling salt to a boil in a medium stainless-steel saucepan. Stir until the salt is dissolved.

Pour the brine over the okra in the jars, leaving ¼ inch of headspace. Follow the instructions for boiling-water canning on page 10. Process the jars for 10 minutes. Let the pickles sit for 1 month before serving.

Yellow Squash Pickles

Of all the pickles I make each summer and hand out as gifts, this is the most requested. A neighbor, the late Doris Avery, once left me a voicemail message raving about the pickles and noting that she had eaten a whole jar by herself in a couple days. I soon delivered a second jar. This recipe is reprinted with permission from Jean Anderson's Preserving Guide: How to Pickle and Preserve, Can and Freeze, Dry and Store Vegetables and Fruits *(Chapel Hill: University of North Carolina Press, 2012).*

MAKES 6–8 PINT JARS

---

12 medium-sized tender young yellow squash,
    cut into 1/4-inch slices
3 dozen small silverskin white onions, sliced very thin
1/2 cup pickling salt
6 cups ice cubes
3 1/2 cups sugar
1 quart white vinegar
1 3/4 teaspoons turmeric
1 3/4 teaspoons celery seeds
1 3/4 teaspoons white mustard seeds

Layer the squash and onions alternately in a very large mixing bowl, sprinkling with pickling salt as you go. Pile ice on top and let stand at room temperature for 3 hours. Place in a colander to drain and rinse well in cool water. Drain well, pressing out as much liquid as possible.

Bring the sugar, vinegar, turmeric, celery seeds, and mustard seeds to a rolling boil over medium heat in a large stainless-steel stockpot or enamel Dutch oven. Add the squash and onions and stir gently. Bring just to the boiling point.

Pack the squash and onions into hot, sterilized jars, leaving 1/4 inch of headspace. Follow the instructions for boiling-water canning on page 10. Process the jars for 10 minutes.

Pickled Peppers Stuffed with Shredded Cabbage

These stuffed peppers have a satisfying sweet-and-sour flavor. We eat them on their own or as part of a pickle plate, but they also make an excellent accompaniment to rich dishes, such as cheese grits, risotto, or anything with lamb. This recipe comes from Anne Lewis Anderson, the stepmother of James Beard Award–winning cookbook author Jean Anderson. Anne was the head of the math department at the University of North Carolina at Greensboro. As one would expect of a math professor, Anne's cookbook notes the number of jars she canned each year. If you can find cherry peppers, use them; if you can't, use small, sweet, red bell peppers, slightly larger than golf balls.

MAKES 2 QUART JARS

1 head of cabbage, finely shredded

3 cups water

3 tablespoons pickling salt

20–22 cherry peppers or small red bell peppers

3 cups white vinegar

4 cups sugar

1 tablespoon plus 1 teaspoon pickling spice

Place the cabbage in a bowl with the water and pickling salt. Stir to dissolve the salt. Let the cabbage sit overnight at room temperature.

The next day, drain and rinse the cabbage several times until the saltiness is to your liking. Stuff each pepper's cavity with shredded cabbage.

Pack the stuffed peppers into hot, sterilized jars. Pack more peppers than you think possible into each jar, but be careful not to tear them.

Combine the vinegar and sugar in a medium saucepan. Place the pickling spice in a large tea strainer or in a layer or two of cheesecloth tied with butcher string. Add it to the vinegar. Bring to a boil, stirring until the sugar is dissolved. Remove the pickling spice.

Pour the syrup over the peppers in the jars, leaving ½ inch of headspace. Follow the instructions for boiling-water canning on page 10. Process the jars for 15 minutes. Let the peppers sit for 1 month before eating.

Pickled Figs

These sweet-and-tart figs are excellent with any pork dish, especially ham or grilled pork chops. This recipe is reprinted with permission from Jean Anderson's Preserving Guide: How to Pickle and Preserve, Can and Freeze, Dry and Store Vegetables and Fruits *(Chapel Hill: University of North Carolina Press, 2012). Jean's recipe calls for "bruising" the whole cloves and allspice. I accomplished that by using the blade of a large chef's knife to smash the cloves and allspice against a cutting board.*

MAKES 8–10 PINT JARS

---

10 pounds firm but ripe figs

1 gallon boiling water

1 quart apple cider vinegar

1 quart cold water

6 cups sugar

2 tablespoons whole cloves, bruised

1 tablespoon whole allspice, bruised

2 cinnamon sticks, each broken in several places

2 long, thin strips of lemon rind, yellow part only

Wash the figs well in cool water and drain; don't stem or peel. To prevent the figs from bursting during processing, prick each once or twice with a sterilized needle. Place the figs in a large bowl, pour in the boiling water, and let stand until the water cools to room temperature. Drain the figs.

Place the vinegar, cold water, and sugar in a large, heavy enamel or stainless-steel pot. Tie the cloves, allspice, cinnamon, and lemon rind loosely in several thicknesses of cheesecloth and drop in the pot. Set the pot over moderate heat and bring to a boil. Add the figs, reduce the heat slightly so the syrup boils gently, then boil for 45 minutes to 1 hour, or until the figs are translucent and tender. Remove the spice bag.

Use a slotted spoon to pack the figs into hot, sterilized jars, arranging them as snugly and attractively as possible. Pour enough of the syrup into the jars to cover the figs, leaving ¼ inch of headspace. Follow the instructions for boiling-water canning on page 10. Process the jars for 15 minutes. Let the figs sit for 1 month before eating.

Best-in-Show Jalapeño Pickles

In 2012, I was asked to judge the pickles and preserves contest at the North Carolina State Fair in Raleigh. I was blown away by the level of canning talent in the state and especially by this Best-in-Show winner from Rebecca Evans of Clayton, North Carolina. Jalapeño lovers will love these pickles.

MAKES 3 PINT JARS

---

8 cups seeded, sliced jalapeños
3 cups sugar
1 tablespoon celery seeds
1 tablespoon mustard seeds
2 cups apple cider vinegar

Cover the jalapeños with boiling water and let stand for 5 minutes.

Combine the sugar, celery seeds, mustard seeds, and vinegar in a medium saucepan. Bring to a boil. Drain the jalapeños and pack into hot, sterilized jars.

Ladle the brine over the jalapeños, leaving ¼ inch of headspace. Follow the instructions for boiling-water canning on page 10. Process the jars for 10 minutes. These pickles are best after sitting for at least 2 weeks.

Green Tomato Pickles

This may be one of the best uses for tomatoes that never seem to ripen before the first fall frost. Once you've had your fill of fried green tomatoes, you can use the last tomatoes on the vine to make these pickles or Green Tomato Relish (page 84). These pickles are standard fare on the pickle plates I set out during oyster roasts, pig pickins, or any holiday meal when we're serving a glazed ham.

MAKES 6 PINT JARS

2½ pounds green tomatoes, quartered
2 medium yellow onions, sliced
1 small red bell pepper, diced
¼ cup finely chopped jalapeños
4½ cups white vinegar
3 cups sugar
2 tablespoons mustard seeds
5 teaspoons black peppercorns
2 teaspoons celery seeds

Place the tomatoes and onions in a large bowl. Dice the bell pepper by hand, then add it to the tomatoes and onions. Feel free to chop the jalapeños, including the seeds, in a food processor, but if you do it by hand, be sure to wear plastic gloves. Add the jalapeños to the tomato mixture. Stir to combine.

Place the vinegar, sugar, mustard seeds, peppercorns, and celery seeds in a medium stainless-steel saucepan. Bring to a boil and stir to dissolve the sugar.

Pack the vegetables into hot, sterilized jars. Fill the jars with the brine, leaving ½ inch of headspace. Follow the boiling-water canning instructions on page 10. Process the jars for 15 minutes. Let the pickles sit for 1 week before enjoying.

Watermelon Rind Pickles

This recipe had to be created during desperate times because it turns something otherwise inedible into something delicious. Trimming the rind from the watermelon's red fruit and peeling the skin is too much trouble unless you're desperate. Today, I only go to the trouble to make these pickles to please a few southern friends who haven't tasted their grandmothers' watermelon rind pickles in years. One night while she was scrounging in her kitchen for something to eat, my friend and fellow food writer Kathleen Purvis of the Charlotte Observer *discovered that these pickles go well with prosciutto.*

I bought a twelve-quart plastic bucket with a lid at a restaurant-supply store to make these pickles, but any food-safe plastic container with a lid will work. When using pickling lime, avoid aluminum containers, colanders, or pots because the lime can react with the metal, increasing the aluminum content of the pickles, according to the National Center for Home Food Preservation at the University of Georgia.

MAKES 8 PINT JARS

12–14-pound watermelon

2 quarts water

3 tablespoons pickling lime

5½ cups apple cider vinegar

3 cups water

10 cups sugar

2-inch piece of fresh ginger, peeled and sliced into 8 pieces

8 cinnamon sticks

Halve the watermelon lengthwise, then quarter each half. Cut into 1-inch slices and remove the red fruit from the rind (you can use it in a fruit salad or daiquiris). Use a vegetable peeler to remove the green skin, leaving only the white rind. Cut the rind into 1 × 1-inch pieces. Add the rind to a large nonreactive food-safe container with a lid with 2 quarts water and the pickling lime. Stir to dissolve the lime, then cover the container with the lid. Let soak overnight.

The next day, drain the rind in a nonreactive colander and rinse. Place the rind in a bowl filled with cool water and let sit for 1 hour. Drain. Repeat the rinsing and soaking twice more.

Put the rind in a large stainless-steel stockpot or enamel Dutch oven and cover with water. Bring to a boil and simmer until just tender and transparent. (This step can be tricky. You want the rind to be tender but not mushy. The best way to test it is to taste it.) When done, drain.

To make the brine, bring the vinegar, 3 cups water, and sugar to a boil in a large pot. Stir to dissolve the sugar. Reduce the heat and simmer until the syrup reaches 220° on a candy thermometer.

Place a slice of ginger and a cinnamon stick in each hot, sterilized jar. Pack the watermelon rind into the jars. Ladle the syrup over the rind, leaving ½ inch of headspace. Follow the instructions for boiling-water canning on page 10. Process the jars for 10 minutes. Let the pickles sit for 1 month before eating.

Mustard Pickle

When I'm craving something pickled, I often find myself fishing the cauliflower florets out of a jar of mustard pickle. I leave the pearl onions for my husband. This recipe is adapted from one that appears in A Gracious Plenty: Recipes and Recollections from the American South, by John T. Edge for the Center for the Study of Southern Culture at the University of Mississippi (New York: G. P. Putnam's Sons, 1999), and the N.C. Governors' Mustard Pickle recipe in Pickles and Preserves, by Marion Brown (Chapel Hill: University of North Carolina Press, 2002).

MAKES 8 PINT JARS

1 (10-ounce) bag white pearl onions

1 large head of cauliflower, cut up into small florets, stems sliced

6 small pickling cucumbers, such as Kirby, diced

1 large green bell pepper, diced

1 large red bell pepper, diced

1 celery stalk, diced

12 cups ice water, plus more if needed

$\frac{1}{2}$ cup pickling salt

1 cup flour

2 cups sugar

1 tablespoon dry mustard

2 teaspoons turmeric

9 cups white vinegar

Fill a small stainless-steel saucepan with water and bring to a boil. Fill a small bowl with ice water. Add the pearl onions to the boiling water. Cook for 2–3 minutes, then use a slotted spoon to remove the onions to the ice-water bath. Peel off the onion skins.

Place the onions, cauliflower, cucumbers, bell peppers, and celery in a large nonreactive container with a lid. (I use a 12-quart plastic container with a lid that I purchased at a restaurant-supply store.)

Add enough ice water to cover the vegetables. Add the pickling salt. Stir to combine. Cover the container with the lid. Let sit for 12–24 hours.

The next day, transfer the vegetables and brine to a large stainless-steel stockpot or enamel Dutch oven. Bring to a boil. Drain the vegetables in a colander and rinse them several times with cold water until the saltiness is to your liking.

Combine the flour, sugar, mustard, and turmeric in a large stainless-steel stockpot or enamel Dutch oven. Mix well. Slowly add the vinegar, stirring until there are no lumps and the mixture is thoroughly combined. Cook over medium heat until thickened, about 4–5 minutes. Add the vegetables to the sauce. Bring back to a boil and cook for about 12 minutes.

Ladle the vegetables and sauce into hot, sterilized jars, leaving ¼ inch of headspace. Follow the boiling-water canning instructions on page 10. Process the jars for 10 minutes. Let the pickles sit for 1 month before eating.

Pickled Beets

I'm always stumped about what to get my brother-in-law, Don Padgett, who lives in Pinehurst, North Carolina, as a gift. Luckily, I discovered during the process of writing this book that he will eat a whole jar of pickled beets in one sitting. So his birthday and holiday gifts for years to come will be these pickled beets. To determine whether the beets are done cooking, taste them to make sure they're tender and not al dente.

MAKES 3 PINT JARS

2½ pounds beets
1 teaspoon salt
1½ cups white vinegar
½ cup water
¾ cup sugar
½ teaspoon whole cloves
1 cinnamon stick

Place the beets in a large pot and cover with water. Add the salt. Bring to a boil and cook until easily pierced with a knife. The cooking time will depend on the size of the beets.

Using a slotted spoon, place the beets on a cutting board until cool enough to handle. Peel the beets and cut into ½-inch slices. Quarter the slices or cut into 6 pieces so they fit more easily into the jars.

Combine the vinegar, water, sugar, cloves, and cinnamon stick in a large saucepan. Cook over medium-high heat, stirring to dissolve the sugar, about 5 minutes. Remove the cinnamon stick and strain out the cloves.

Pack the beets into hot, sterilized jars. Pour the brine over the beets, leaving ¼ inch of headspace. Follow the instructions for boiling-water canning on page 10. Process the jars for 10 minutes. Let the beets sit for 1 month before eating.

Jerusalem Artichoke Pickles

Jerusalem artichokes, also called sunchokes, are native perennial sunflowers that grow from Maine to Texas. The roots are tubers and can be adapted to many recipes that call for potatoes. They keep best in the ground, so just dig up the tubers when you need them after the tall, gangly flowers have died back. These unusual pickles are a nice addition to a pickle plate. I don't bother to peel mine; I just cut them into bite-size chunks after a good scrubbing. If you prefer a prettier pickle, do as Matt and Ted Lee suggest in The Lee Bros. Charleston Kitchen *(New York: Clarkson Potter, 2013): peel the tubers and cut into ¼-inch slices on a mandolin.*

MAKES 7 PINT JARS

3½ pounds Jerusalem artichokes

5 cups apple cider vinegar

1¾ cups water

2½ cups brown sugar

3 tablespoons salt

2 tablespoons black peppercorns

14 dried chili peppers, such as árbol

Scrub the dirt out of the nooks and crannies of the Jerusalem artichokes. Trim any damaged or soft spots. Dry the Jerusalem artichokes completely and cut into bite-size pieces.

Combine the vinegar, water, brown sugar, salt, and peppercorns in a large stainless-steel stockpot or enamel Dutch oven. Bring to a boil over medium heat.

Pack the Jerusalem artichokes into hot, sterilized jars and add 2 chili peppers to each jar. Ladle enough brine over the artichokes to leave ½ inch of headspace. Follow the boiling-water canning instructions on page 10. Process the jars for 15 minutes. Let the pickles sit for 2 weeks before enjoying.

Relishes, Chutneys, and More

This chapter shows off the relishes, chutneys, and salsas that are part of many southern canners' repertoires. Who can resist trying a recipe nicknamed Crack Cocaine Relish? Not me. Then there are the intriguing oddball recipes. The Spiced Grapes recipe transforms muscadines into a spicy condiment that's perfect for venison or pork. Brandied Peaches make a delicious boozy topping for ice cream, and the syrup becomes an endless source of cocktail inspirations.

Brandied Peaches

These peaches are delicious over ice cream or alongside a slice of pound cake. My first batch was a bit too boozy, but it livened up my friend Debbie Moose's book club one evening. I've reduced the amount of brandy since then, but feel free to increase it if you prefer or replace the brandy with a good-quality bourbon. Consider using the syrup to liven up a glass of inexpensive sparkling white wine or as an ingredient in other cocktails.

MAKES 2 WIDE-MOUTH QUART JARS

Juice of 1 large lemon or 1 teaspoon Fruit Fresh
   Produce Protector
10–12 small, ripe clingstone peaches
6 cups sugar
6 cups water
Good-quality brandy

Fill a large stainless-steel stockpot or enamel Dutch oven with water and bring to a boil. Have a large bowl of ice water mixed with lemon juice or Fruit Fresh ready nearby.

Once the water on the stove is boiling, gently drop a few peaches at a time into the pot. When the peach skin "shrugs" to the touch after a few minutes, use a slotted spoon to remove the peach to the ice-water bath. If the skin doesn't loosen after a few minutes, remove the peach and peel it with a vegetable peeler when it's cool enough to handle. Repeat with the remaining peaches. Keep the peeled peaches in the bowl of ice water.

Combine the sugar and water in a large stainless-steel stockpot or enamel Dutch oven over medium-low heat. Bring to a simmer. Stir until the sugar is dissolved. Add the peaches, in batches if necessary. Cook until the peaches are tender, about 15 minutes. Use a skewer to test doneness; the skewer should easily pierce the fruit. Use a slotted spoon to remove the peaches to a large platter.

Continue simmering the syrup until it reaches 220° on a candy thermometer. Pack the peaches into hot, sterilized jars.

Ladle enough syrup into each jar to fill it two-thirds of the way full. Fill the jars the rest of the way with brandy, leaving ½ inch of headspace. Follow the instructions for boiling-water canning on page 10. Process the jars for 10 minutes. The peaches will be ready to enjoy in 4–6 weeks.

Spiced Grapes

This recipe turns those musky muscadine grapes into spiced pre-serves that make an excellent condiment for grilled venison or pork.

MAKES 4 HALF-PINT JARS

1½ pounds muscadine grapes
1 cup water, plus more if needed
1 cup white vinegar
2⅓ cups sugar
⅛ teaspoon ground cloves
½ teaspoon cinnamon
½ teaspoon allspice

Separate the grape skins from the pulp by popping the grapes between your thumb and index finger. Place the pulp with the seeds in a medium bowl and the skin in a medium stainless-steel saucepan. Remove the seeds from the pulp, making several passes since it's hard to remove all the seeds on the first attempt.

Add the water to the skins in the saucepan. Cook over medium-high heat, about 30 minutes, or until the skins are tender. Stir occasionally. You may need to add more water, ½ cup at a time, to prevent scorching. When the skins are tender, transfer to a food processor and pulse until finely chopped. Return the puréed skins to the saucepan.

Use a food mill or food processor to pulverize the pulp or push the pulp through a fine mesh strainer with the back of a wooden spoon. Add the pulp to the saucepan, then add the vinegar, sugar, cloves, cinnamon, and allspice. Cook the grapes over medium-high heat until the temperature registers 220° on a candy thermometer.

Fill hot, sterilized jars with the grapes. Follow the instructions for boiling-water canning on page 10. Process the jars for 10 minutes. Let the grapes sit for 1 month before serving.

Peach-Tomato Salsa

This fruity salsa is great served with chips or as a topping for grilled fish tacos. The recipe comes from Andrea Ashby, an avid canner who lives in Raleigh, North Carolina. She uses her food processor to mince the jalapeños and garlic. She recommends using freestone peaches because they're easier to pit.

MAKES 6 PINT JARS

8 cups peeled, diced tomatoes
8 cups peeled, diced peaches
4 cups seeded, diced jalapeños
4 cups chopped onion
16 garlic cloves, minced
1 cup chopped cilantro
2 tablespoons salt
1½ cups apple cider vinegar
1½ cups fresh lime juice

Combine all ingredients in a large stainless-steel stockpot or enamel Dutch oven. Bring to a boil and cook for 10 minutes.

Ladle the salsa into hot, sterilized jars, leaving ½ inch of headspace. Follow the instructions for boiling-water canning on page 10. Process the jars for 15 minutes. Let the salsa sit for 1 month before enjoying.

Quick Pickled-Cucumber Salsa

Cookbook author Sandra Gutierrez, a master of Latin American cuisine, shared this salsa recipe with me. She serves this salsa as a dip for tortilla chips or a topping for grilled salmon or fried catfish.

MAKES 8 SERVINGS

FOR THE SALSA

4 cups English cucumbers, seeded and finely chopped
2 cups seeded, finely chopped plum tomatoes
1½ cups finely chopped Vidalia onion
1½ cups finely chopped red bell pepper
2 jalapeños, seeded and minced

FOR THE DRESSING

1 cup roughly chopped cilantro (leaves and tender stems)
3 green onions (white and light green parts only)
⅓ cup fresh lemon juice
2 teaspoons honey
¼ cup extra-virgin olive oil
Salt and freshly ground black pepper, to taste

In a large bowl, combine the cucumbers, tomatoes, onion, bell pepper, and jalapeños.

In a blender, place the cilantro, green onions, lemon juice, and honey; blend at high speed for 1 minute, or until the mixture is smooth. With the motor running, drizzle the olive oil in a thin stream through the feeding tube and blend for an additional 20 seconds, or until the mixture has changed from dark green to light green (it won't emulsify into a thick dressing but will remain loose). Season with salt and pepper. Pour the dressing over the salsa; toss well to coat.

Chill the salsa, tossing periodically, for 1 hour, in order for the vegetables to pickle.

Sweet Pepper Relish

This relish has many uses in the kitchen. You can add it to egg salad, potato salad, or even meatloaf mix. You can garnish deviled eggs with it, spoon some over a block of cream cheese and serve it with crackers, or mix it with sour cream to make a dip for chips. For relishes, I prefer to chop the vegetables by hand because I find the food processor can turn relish ingredients into a purée in no time. But if you have better luck with your food processor, take advantage of the convenience.

MAKES 4 HALF-PINT JARS

1 pound yellow onions, diced
1 medium red bell pepper, diced
2 medium orange bell peppers, diced
3 banana peppers, diced
3 jalapeños, seeded and finely diced
¾ cup white vinegar
1 cup sugar
1½ teaspoons pickling salt

Place the onions, peppers, and jalapeños in a large stainless-steel stockpot or enamel Dutch oven. Add the vinegar, sugar, and salt. Bring to a simmer over medium-low heat. Stir to dissolve the sugar and salt. Cook about 30 minutes, or until the liquid is almost gone.

Pack the relish into hot, sterilized jars, leaving ¼ inch of headspace. Follow the instructions for boiling-water canning on page 10. Process the jars for 10 minutes.

Vegetable Relish

Friend and cookbook author Debbie Moose shared this recipe with me, with this comment: "Friends and I get together each summer to make dozens of jars of this relish, which we've dubbed 'Crack Cocaine Relish' for its addictive qualities. People go nuts over it and beg for more. I think it's because it's not too sweet, not too tart, and doesn't have cabbage, which I don't like in a relish or chow-chow. It's great on turkey sandwiches, burgers, or cooked beans or in deviled eggs."

MAKES 4 PINT JARS

3 pounds tomatoes, peeled and cut into chunks

3 pounds zucchini, cut into strips

3 large red bell peppers, cut into strips

3 large green bell peppers, cut into strips

4 small cayenne peppers or 1 large hot banana pepper, seeded and quartered

2 large onions, cut into chunks

4 garlic cloves

$\frac{1}{4}$ cup pickling salt

$2\frac{1}{2}$ cups white vinegar

2 cups sugar

1 heaping teaspoon dried thyme, crushed

$\frac{1}{2}$ teaspoon freshly ground black pepper

Use the food-grinder attachment of a stand mixer or a hand-crank meat grinder to grind together the tomatoes, zucchini, peppers, onions, and garlic. Don't use a food processor because it will purée the vegetables.

Place the vegetables in a nonmetallic container and sprinkle with the pickling salt. Cover and refrigerate overnight.

The next day, place the mixture in a large colander over the sink, rinse well, and drain thoroughly. Combine the vinegar, sugar, thyme, and pepper in a large Dutch oven or saucepan. Bring the mixture to a boil, stirring to dissolve the sugar. Add the vegetables and return to a boil, then remove the pan from the heat.

Ladle the mixture into hot, sterilized jars, leaving ¼ inch of headspace. Follow the instructions for boiling-water canning on page 10. Process the jars for 10 minutes. You can enjoy this relish immediately, but it's better after sitting a couple of weeks.

Corn and Sweet Pepper Relish

I am blessed to live in an area of the South populated by many food writers who have graciously shared recipes for this book. Among them is Sheri Castle, author of the The New Southern Garden Cookbook *(Chapel Hill: University of North Carolina Press, 2011). Sheri is known for teaching classes at the Carrboro Farmers' Market, a local institution that has made an effort to teach its customers how to preserve food. This is a recipe from one of Sheri's popular classes. Sheri uses this relish as a side dish, a dip for tortilla chips, a sauce for grilled meats, or a topping for black beans or fish tacos.*

MAKES 6 PINT JARS

4 cups white vinegar

1½ cups sugar

2 teaspoons pickling salt or iodine-free kosher salt

2 teaspoons dry mustard

1 teaspoon celery seeds

1 teaspoon turmeric

½ teaspoon cayenne pepper, or to taste

2 teaspoons coriander seeds

8 cups corn kernels

4 cups finely diced onion

4½ cups finely diced sweet bell pepper, any color

2 tablespoons ClearJel or 3 tablespoons cornstarch
dissolved in 2 tablespoons cold water (don't use the water
if you use the ClearJel), optional

Chowchow

My friend Kathleen Purvis, food editor at the Charlotte Observer, *calls this classic relish southern kimchi. Kathleen wrote in a 2011 article that chowchow is also known as chow-chow, chow chow, piccalilli, even end-of-the-season relish. It's typically made with what's left in the garden before the first frost: green tomatoes, cabbage, peppers, and onions. Other ingredients can sneak into chowchow as well: carrots, cauliflower, and zucchini. Enjoy a tablespoon of this relish on hot dogs, hamburgers, or pinto beans. You can also add it to potato salad, macaroni salad, chicken salad, or egg salad. I use a mandolin to make quick work of shredding and dicing the cabbage, onion, and jalapeños. If you like a hotter relish, increase the number of jalapeños.*

MAKES 9 PINT JARS

6 green tomatoes, diced

2 medium heads cabbage, shredded

1 large yellow onion, diced

1 small green bell pepper, diced

1 small red bell pepper, diced

2–3 jalapeños, seeded and diced

¼ cup pickling salt

2 cups water

6 cups white vinegar

2 cups sugar

2 tablespoons celery seeds

1 tablespoon mustard seeds

2 teaspoons ground mustard

2 teaspoons turmeric

Place the tomatoes, cabbage, onion, bell peppers, and jalapeños in a large nonreactive container with a lid. (I use a 12-quart plastic bucket with a lid that I purchased at a restaurant-supply store.) Add enough ice water to cover the vegetables and add the pickling salt. Stir, cover with a lid, and let sit for 12–24 hours.

The next day, drain and rinse the vegetables in a colander several times until the saltiness is to your liking.

Place the vegetables in a large stainless-steel stockpot or enamel Dutch oven. Add the water, vinegar, sugar, celery seeds, mustard seeds, ground mustard, and turmeric. Bring the mixture to a boil.

Pack the chowchow into hot, sterilized jars, leaving ¼ inch of headspace. Follow the boiling-water canning instructions on page 10. Process the jars for 10 minutes. Let the relish sit for 1 month before eating.

Green Tomato Relish

This sweet, salty relish is good on field peas, burgers, hot dogs, and more. When a relish recipe calls for letting the vegetables sit in a salt brine overnight, like this one does, I recommend rinsing the mixture as many times as needed, tasting it after each rinse, until you like the degree of saltiness.

MAKES 3 PINT JARS

4 pounds large green tomatoes
2 medium red bell peppers, diced
1 large green bell pepper, diced
2 medium onions, diced
2 jalapeños, diced
¼ cup pickling salt
2 cups apple cider vinegar
1¾ cups sugar
1 tablespoon pickling spice

Bring a large pot filled with water to a boil on the stove. Fill a large bowl with ice water.

Drop the green tomatoes, a few at a time, into the boiling water and boil for 3 minutes. Remove with a slotted spoon to the ice bath. Use your fingers to peel off the skins; if they aren't loose enough, use a vegetable peeler.

Quarter the peeled tomatoes. Remove the pulpy middle and discard. Chop the outer shell of the tomato into ¼-inch pieces, about the size of a hot dog relish. Place the diced tomatoes in a large nonreactive plastic container with a lid. Add the diced bell peppers and onions.

You can use a food processor to dice the jalapeños, including the seeds. If you dice them by hand, wear plastic gloves. Add the jalapeños to the other vegetables. Add the pickling salt, stir to combine, and cover with a lid. Let sit overnight.

The next day, drain and rinse the vegetable mixture in a colander until the saltiness is to your liking. Press out the liquid.

In a large stainless-steel stockpot or enamel Dutch oven, combine the vinegar, sugar, and pickling spice. Bring a boil, stirring to dissolve the sugar. Add the vegetables and return to a boil. Lower the heat and let the mixture simmer for 15 minutes.

Pack the relish into hot, sterilized jars, leaving ¼ inch of headspace. Follow the instructions for boiling-water canning on page 10. Process the jars for 10 minutes. Let the relish sit for 1 week before enjoying.

Sauerkraut

I have to say that the prospect of making sauerkraut scared me at first. I had no idea it was so simple. It's best to use fresh cabbage bought directly from a farmer. Freshly picked cabbage releases more water, creating its own juice for fermentation. If you use store-bought cabbage, you may have to supplement whatever liquid you get from the cabbage. Add enough brine to cover the shredded cabbage. While the smell of homemade sauerkraut may turn you off, the key is to rinse it with water before cooking or serving it. This kraut goes well with hot dogs, bratwurst, kielbasa, and roasted pork.

MAKES ABOUT 7 CUPS

1 large head of cabbage
3 tablespoons pickling salt, plus more if needed
Water, if needed

Discard the outer leaves of the cabbage. Core the cabbage and use a mandolin to thinly slice or shred it into a large nonreactive container with a lid. Add the pickling salt and toss to thoroughly coat the cabbage. Cover with a lid and let sit overnight.

The next day, check to see if the cabbage has released enough liquid to cover itself when weighed down with plates. If not, make a brine using 1½ tablespoons pickling salt for every quart of water. Add enough of the brine to cover the cabbage. Then weigh down the cabbage with plates so it's completely submerged.

Store the container of fermenting cabbage at 70°–75° for 4–6 weeks, skimming off any funky sludge or scum every couple of days.

Once the kraut has stopped bubbling, it's fully fermented and can be stored in the refrigerator for several months or canned. To can it, fill clean jars with the kraut and brine, leaving ½ inch of headspace. Follow the instructions for boiling-water canning on page 10. Process pint jars for 20 minutes and quart jars for 25 minutes.

Jerusalem Artichoke Relish

I grow a patch of Jerusalem artichokes, also called sunchokes, in my backyard. The second year I harvested them, I had more than I could possibly use. I found a willing taker in the James Beard Award–winning chef Ben Barker, who along with his pastry chef wife, Karen, owned the now-closed Magnolia Grill in Durham, North Carolina. (It should be noted that Karen has her own James Beard Award.) In exchange for the artichokes, Ben shared this relish recipe with me. Be sure to clean the artichokes with a scrub brush to remove all of the dirt and cut off any damaged or soft spots. This relish is a nice crunchy addition to potato salad, egg salad, or macaroni salad and is also a good topping for a bowl of pinto beans or field peas.

MAKES 7 PINT JARS

1 gallon plus 2 cups cold water, divided

1½ cups kosher salt, divided

3½ pounds Jerusalem artichokes, scrubbed, trimmed, and diced

2 cups diced red bell pepper

2 cups diced yellow bell pepper

2 cups diced onion

2 cups granulated sugar

1 cup light brown sugar

5 cups apple cider vinegar

2 tablespoons plus 2 teaspoons mustard seeds

2 teaspoons red pepper flakes

2 tablespoons turmeric

Place 1 gallon cold water and 1 cup salt in a large bowl. Stir to dissolve the salt. Add the artichokes. Soak overnight or at least for 5–6 hours. Rinse and drain well.

Place the bell peppers, onion, ½ cup salt, and 2 cups water in another large bowl. Let soak for 1 hour. Rinse, drain, and combine with the artichokes.

Combine the sugars, vinegar, mustard seeds, red pepper flakes, and turmeric in a stainless-steel saucepan. Bring to a simmer and cook gently for 2 minutes. Pour over the artichoke mixture. Let cool to room temperature.

Pack in the hot, sterilized jars, leaving ¼ inch of headspace. Follow the instructions for boiling-water canning on page 10. Process the jars for 10 minutes. Let sit for at least 2 weeks before enjoying.

Gammaw's Marinated Carrots

Gammaw is the nickname of Kathleen Purvis's maternal grand-mother. Kathleen is a dear friend and the food editor at the Char-lotte Observer. *These refrigerator-marinated carrots are also known as copper pennies. The recipe can be found in many church or community cookbooks. I've made it using precut baby carrots with good results. I like having a jar of these in the refrigerator. They make an easy side dish on a busy weeknight when I'm trying to pull dinner together with a toddler attached to my legs.*

MAKES 2 QUART JARS

- 2 pounds carrots, cut into 1/3-inch slices
- 1 teaspoon salt
- 1 cup sugar
- 3/4 cup apple cider vinegar
- 1/2 cup vegetable oil
- 1 teaspoon ground mustard
- 1 teaspoon freshly ground black pepper
- 1 teaspoon Worcestershire sauce
- 1 (10.75-ounce) can condensed tomato soup
- 1 large onion, thinly sliced
- 1 large green bell pepper, diced

Place the carrots in a large stainless-steel saucepan filled with salted water. Cook over medium-low heat until tender, 10–12 minutes. Drain well.

Combine the salt, sugar, vinegar, oil, mustard, pepper, Worcestershire sauce, and tomato soup in a large bowl. Stir until the salt and sugar are dissolved.

Add the carrots, onion, and bell pepper. Stir to saturate the vegetables. Pack the vegetables and sauce into clean jars and seal with lids. These carrots will keep in the refrigerator for up to 6 weeks.

Cranberry-Apple Chutney

For Jill Warren Lucas of Raleigh, North Carolina, a Thanksgiving meal is not complete unless it includes this chutney. But don't wait for the holiday to try it. Its tangy sweetness is delicious on a turkey sandwich, in a grilled cheese sandwich, or served alongside grilled pork chops. It's also great drizzled over a block of cream cheese and nibbled with crackers.

MAKES 12 HALF-PINT JARS

- 1 cup brown sugar
- 2 cups granulated sugar
- 1 cup water
- 6 tablespoons fresh lemon juice
- ½ cup apple cider vinegar
- 2 teaspoons kosher salt
- 1 teaspoon cinnamon
- ½ teaspoon ginger
- 6 cups fresh cranberries
- 1 cup chopped celery
- 1 cup chopped Honeycrisp apples (or other tart, crisp variety)
- 1 cup golden raisins
- ½ cup chopped walnuts

Place the sugars, water, lemon juice, vinegar, salt, cinnamon, and ginger in a large stainless-steel stockpot or enamel Dutch oven. Bring to a simmer over medium heat and stir to combine. Increase the heat to medium-high and add the cranberries, celery, apples, raisins, and walnuts. Bring to a boil and stir often for about 15 minutes, or until the cranberries have popped and the mixture starts to thicken. It should still be slightly wet and loose when done.

Ladle the chutney into hot, sterilized jars, leaving ½ inch of headspace. Follow the instructions for boiling-water canning on page 10. Process the jars for 10 minutes.

Peach Chutney

This sweet, hot chutney recipe comes from Marilyn Markel, who runs a cooking school at Southern Season's Charleston, South Carolina, location. Southern Season is a chain of gourmet food and housewares stores that started in Chapel Hill, North Carolina. If you like a hotter chutney, feel free to increase the number of jalapeños. Marilyn uses it to glaze chicken, as a condiment for grilled pork or fried chicken, or on sweet potato biscuits topped with pulled pork.

MAKES 8 PINT JARS

---

2 cups sugar

2 cups apple cider vinegar

6 pounds peeled, sliced peaches

2 large garlic cloves, minced

2 tablespoons fresh ginger, peeled and grated

¼ cup finely chopped onion

2 tablespoons salt

⅓ cup crystallized ginger

⅓ cup dried currants

Zest of 1 lime

4 small jalapeños, seeded and finely diced

Bring the sugar and vinegar to a boil in a large stainless-steel stockpot or enamel Dutch oven. Stir until the sugar is dissolved.

Add the peaches, garlic, fresh ginger, onion, salt, crystallized ginger, currants, lime zest, and jalapeños and cook over low heat for 1–1½ hours, or until thick. Stir often.

Ladle the chutney into hot, sterilized jars, leaving ½ inch of headspace. Follow the instructions for boiling-water canning on page 10. Process the jars for 10 minutes.

Acknowledgments

I live in a wonderful community of writers, chefs, and food entrepreneurs.

Thanks to Jean Anderson, a grande dame among cookbook authors, who answered my questions, helped me work through problems, and offered feedback on the numerous jars of pickles and preserves that I left on her doorstep.

Thanks to the many talented cookbook authors, food writers, editors, and others who offered suggestions, gave feedback, and even shared recipes: Andrea Ashby, Rebecca Ashby, Ben Barker, Karen Barker, Sheri Castle, Greg Cox, Rebecca Evans, Ben Fillipio, Damon Lee Fowler, Felicia Gressette, Sandra Gutierrez, Jill Warren Lucas, Marilyn Markel, April McGreger, Debbie Moose, Amber Nimocks, Kathleen Purvis, Andrea Reusing, John Roby, Nancy Smith, Fred Thompson, Lynn Truslow, Cheryl Whisenant, Ralph Whisenant, and Grace Young. I am also grateful to those who went into the kitchen to verify that these recipes worked: David Auerbach, Jean Fisher Brinkley, Alex Howard, Sarah Ovaska, and Cat Warren. Thanks also to the many members of the Countryside Garden Club who donated canning jars for this endeavor, especially Sue Tucker.

I also appreciate the support of my family: my sister, Gabrielle Padgett, who babysat and helped peel watermelon for yet another pickle recipe; my mother, Goldie Weigl, who, despite her seventy-two years, spent a week in a steamy kitchen making batch after batch of pickles and preserves; and my husband, Matt Ehlers, who not only encouraged me to tackle this book but also supported me during the many hours of testing and writing.

Finally, thanks to Elaine Maisner, who gave me the opportunity to write my first cookbook, and all the wonderful folks at the University of North Carolina Press.

Index